Mastering the Art of Showing Not Telling in Creative Writing

By
Edward Ellison

Contents

Introduction

What Is "Show, Don't Tell"?

"Show, don't tell" is a fundamental principle in creative writing that encourages writers to engage readers by presenting details through vivid imagery, actions, and dialogue rather than outright stating facts or emotions. This approach allows readers to experience the story and infer its deeper meaning, fostering a more immersive and emotionally resonant reading experience. While it may sound simple, mastering this technique is both an art and a skill that requires practice and intentionality.

Explanation of the Principle

At its core, "show, don't tell" emphasizes demonstration over declaration. Instead of telling the reader that a character is angry, a writer might describe the character's clenched fists, flushed face, and sharp tone of voice. Rather than stating that a setting is eerie, a writer might paint a picture of the long shadows stretching across cracked pavement or the hollow echo of footsteps in an empty alleyway.

The power of "showing" lies in its ability to create a vivid mental image for the reader. By presenting sensory details and actions, writers provide the raw materials for readers to construct their own understanding of the scene, characters, and emotions. This active participation makes the reading experience more engaging and memorable.

For example:

- **Telling:** Sarah was nervous about her presentation.

- **Showing:** Sarah's hands trembled as she adjusted the microphone, her pulse pounding in her ears as she scanned the room full of expectant faces.

Notice how the "showing" example uses specific sensory details and actions to convey Sarah's nervousness. The reader can feel her anxiety without being explicitly told how she feels.

Why It Is Important in Creative Writing

1. **Engages the Reader's Imagination** When writers "show," they invite readers to visualize and interpret the story. This collaborative process engages the reader's imagination, making the narrative more compelling and personal. Instead of passively absorbing information, readers actively connect with the material, deepening their investment in the story.

2. **Creates Emotional Impact** Showing allows readers to experience emotions rather than merely learning about them. For example, describing a grieving character's tear-streaked face and trembling voice creates a stronger emotional connection than simply stating, "He was sad." Readers are more likely to empathize with characters when they can observe their struggles and triumphs firsthand.

3. **Builds Immersion and Atmosphere** Vivid imagery and well-chosen details can transport readers into the story's world. By showing the environment through sensory details—the sound of rain tapping against a window, the metallic tang of blood in the air, or the warmth of a crackling fire—writers can

immerse readers in the setting and mood of the narrative.

4. **Develops Characters Naturally** Showing reveals characters through their actions, speech, and choices rather than through exposition. This approach allows readers to infer personality traits and motivations organically, creating multidimensional characters who feel authentic and relatable. For instance, instead of stating that a character is generous, showing them sharing their last meal with a stranger demonstrates this trait in a tangible way.

5. **Enhances Pacing and Tension** By breaking up exposition with dynamic scenes and active descriptions, showing helps maintain a sense of movement and urgency in the story. It also allows writers to build tension and suspense by revealing information gradually, encouraging readers to keep turning the pages.

Common Misconceptions

Despite its importance, the concept of "show, don't tell" is often misunderstood or misapplied. Here are some common misconceptions:

1. **Misconception: Showing Means Including Every Detail** Some writers believe that showing requires them to describe every aspect of a scene in painstaking detail. In reality, effective showing involves selecting key details that evoke the desired emotion or imagery. Overloading a scene with excessive description can overwhelm readers and slow the pacing.

For example:

- o **Ineffective Showing:** The table was wooden, with a rough surface that bore scratches from years of use. There were four chairs around it, each with slightly worn upholstery. The sunlight streamed through the window, casting a warm glow on the faded tablecloth.

- o **Effective Showing:** The table's scratched surface caught the morning sunlight, each mark a testament to years of family meals and late-night conversations.

The second example uses fewer details but still conveys a vivid image and emotional resonance.

2. **Misconception: Telling Is Always Bad** While "show, don't tell" is a valuable guideline, there are times when telling is more effective or appropriate. For example, summarizing mundane actions or providing background information can help maintain the story's pacing. The key is knowing when to show and when to tell.

For example:

- o **Telling for Efficiency:** Over the next week, the team prepared for the competition, practicing late into the night.

- o **Showing for Emotional Impact:** On the final night of practice, Sarah's voice cracked as she shouted encouragement, her eyes rimmed with exhaustion but blazing with determination.

The first sentence summarizes a period of time, while the second focuses on a pivotal moment that requires emotional depth.

3. **Misconception: Showing Always Requires Dialogue** While dialogue can be an effective way to show character traits and relationships, it is not the only tool available. Writers can also show through actions, internal thoughts, body language, and sensory details. For example:

   o **Action:** He slammed the door behind him, his jaw clenched tight as he paced the room.

   o **Internal Thought:** She tried to steady her breathing, the words of her mentor echoing in her mind: "You've got this."

4. **Misconception: Showing Is Only About Description** Showing goes beyond visual descriptions to encompass all five senses, as well as subtext and context. A character's silence in a tense moment can speak volumes, as can the absence of familiar sounds or smells in a setting.

For example:

   o **Description:** The wind howled through the trees, rattling the shutters.

   o **Subtext:** She sat in the silent room, her fingers tracing the outline of the missing photograph.

Both examples "show" through different techniques, highlighting the versatility of the principle.

5. **Misconception: Showing Requires Flowery Language** Some writers mistakenly equate showing with elaborate or poetic prose. However, effective showing is about clarity and precision, not ornamentation. The goal is to create vivid and meaningful images that enhance the story, not to impress readers with fancy language.

For example:

- o **Ineffective Showing:** The ethereal light of the crescent moon bathed the glistening dewdrops in a silvery embrace.

- o **Effective Showing:** The crescent moon cast a faint glow on the dew-covered grass, each droplet catching the light like a tiny gem.

The second example is more straightforward but still evocative.

Conclusion

"Show, don't tell" is a cornerstone of creative writing that challenges authors to engage readers by evoking rather than explaining. By using vivid imagery, sensory details, and actions, writers can create immersive worlds, authentic characters, and emotionally resonant stories. Understanding when and how to apply this principle—while avoiding common misconceptions—is key to mastering the craft of storytelling. As with any writing technique, practice and experimentation are essential to developing the ability to show effectively and with purpose.

Why Writers Struggle with This Concept

The concept of "show, don't tell" is one of the most emphasized yet challenging principles in creative writing. While its benefits are clear, many writers find it difficult to consistently apply this technique in their work. Several factors contribute to this struggle, including a fear of under-explaining, a tendency to overwrite, and a lack of confidence in readers' ability to infer meaning. By understanding these obstacles, writers can identify and address the issues that hinder their storytelling and work towards mastering this essential skill.

Fear of Under-Explaining

One of the primary reasons writers struggle with "show, don't tell" is a fear of under-explaining. This fear often stems from a desire to ensure that readers fully understand the narrative, the characters, and their motivations. Writers may worry that if they do not explicitly state certain details, the reader will miss or misinterpret the intended meaning. As a result, they may fall into the trap of over-relying on exposition and telling rather than trusting the reader to grasp the nuances of the story through showing.

The Origins of the Fear

The fear of under-explaining often begins with a writer's own experiences as a reader. Many writers, especially those early in their careers, are acutely aware of moments in books where they felt lost or confused due to insufficient explanation. This awareness can lead to a hyper-vigilance in their own writing, where they overcompensate to avoid leaving readers in the dark. Additionally, feedback from beta readers or editors can sometimes reinforce this fear. Comments like "I didn't understand why the character did this" or "This part wasn't clear" may prompt writers to add more exposition than necessary in an attempt to preempt similar critiques.

The Consequences of Over-Explaining

When writers give in to the fear of under-explaining, they risk alienating readers through overly explicit writing. For example, instead of letting a character's dialogue or actions reveal their personality, the writer might insert a sentence like, "John was a kind and generous man who always put others' needs before his own." While this tells the reader who John is, it does not allow them to experience his kindness firsthand. This approach can make the writing feel flat and less engaging, as readers are denied the opportunity to form their own connections with the characters and story.

Overcoming the Fear

To overcome the fear of under-explaining, writers must learn to trust their readers. Readers are often more perceptive than writers give them credit for, and well-placed details and subtext can go a long way in conveying meaning. Instead of spelling everything out, writers can focus on providing clues that guide the reader's understanding. For example, showing John offering his coat to a shivering stranger is far more effective than simply stating that he is generous. By practicing restraint and allowing readers to engage actively with the narrative, writers can strike a balance between clarity and subtlety.

Tendency to Overwrite

Another common struggle for writers is the tendency to overwrite when attempting to "show" rather than "tell." In their effort to provide vivid descriptions and immerse readers in the story, writers may include excessive detail or overly elaborate language. This can lead to bloated prose that slows down the pacing and overwhelms the reader.

Why Writers Overwrite

The tendency to overwrite often stems from a genuine desire to create rich, evocative scenes. Writers may feel that they need to describe every aspect of a setting or character to achieve the level of immersion they're aiming for. However, this well-intentioned effort can backfire if the descriptions become too dense or distract from the core of the story.

Another reason writers overwrite is a lack of confidence in their ability to convey meaning concisely. They may feel that if they do not include every detail, their writing will lack depth or fail to resonate with readers. In some cases, overwriting can also be a symptom of indecision, as writers attempt to cover all bases by including multiple layers of description, even when only one or two are necessary.

Examples of Overwriting

Consider the following example of overwriting:

The crimson-hued curtains, heavy with dust, hung in uneven folds, their edges frayed from years of neglect. The sunlight streaming through the grimy window cast a hazy golden glow on the worn wooden floor, where scratches and scuffs told the story of countless footsteps.

While this description paints a vivid picture, it is weighed down by unnecessary detail. The reader might lose interest before reaching the end of the sentence. A more concise version might read:

Dusty crimson curtains framed the grimy window, sunlight casting a golden glow on the scratched wooden floor.

The revised version retains the essential details while eliminating excess, allowing the scene to flow more smoothly.

Avoiding Overwriting

To avoid overwriting, writers should focus on selecting the most impactful details and leaving out the rest. Asking questions like "What does the reader need to know?" and "What detail best captures the mood or tone of this scene?" can help prioritize information. Additionally, writers should resist the urge to impress readers with elaborate language and instead aim for clarity and precision. Reading work aloud or seeking feedback from trusted readers can also help identify areas where the prose feels heavy-handed.

Lack of Confidence in Readers' Ability to Infer

A third reason writers struggle with "show, don't tell" is a lack of confidence in their readers' ability to infer meaning. Writers may feel that unless they spell everything out, readers will miss important nuances or fail to grasp the significance of certain details. This lack of trust can lead to over-explaining and redundant writing that diminishes the reader's engagement.

The Roots of This Lack of Confidence

This lack of confidence often stems from a misunderstanding of the reader-writer relationship. Writers may assume that readers approach their work with less attention or curiosity than they actually do. In reality, most readers are eager to connect the dots and appreciate subtle storytelling. However, writers who have received feedback indicating confusion or misinterpretation may become overly cautious, erring on the side of telling to ensure their point is clear.

The Impact on Writing

When writers do not trust their readers, their writing can become overly didactic. For example, instead of allowing a character's actions to reveal their emotions, the writer might add an explanatory sentence like, "She felt angry and betrayed." This approach not only undermines the emotional impact of the scene but also underestimates the reader's ability to interpret the character's feelings based on context.

Building Trust in Readers

To build confidence in readers' ability to infer, writers should practice incorporating subtext and relying on context to convey meaning. Subtext allows writers to suggest rather than state, leaving room for readers to draw their own conclusions. For example, instead of stating that a character is nervous, a writer might describe their fidgeting hands or darting eyes. These subtle cues invite readers to engage with the text and uncover its layers of meaning.

Additionally, writers should remember that part of the joy of reading comes from discovery. When readers are given the opportunity to infer, they become active participants in the story, which enhances their overall experience. Writers can embrace this dynamic by trusting their audience to pick up on the cues embedded in the narrative.

Conclusion

The struggle to master "show, don't tell" is a common challenge for writers, but understanding the underlying reasons for this difficulty can help address it. By overcoming the fear of under-explaining, avoiding the tendency to overwrite, and building confidence in readers' ability to infer, writers can create stories that are both engaging and impactful. Like any skill, mastering this technique requires practice, feedback, and a willingness to experiment. With time and effort, writers can learn to balance clarity and subtlety, crafting narratives that resonate deeply with their audience.

How This Book Will Help

The principle of "show, don't tell" is vital to creating compelling, immersive stories, but mastering it can be challenging. This book is designed to equip writers with practical tools, concrete examples, and exercises tailored to all levels of experience. Whether you're a beginner seeking foundational techniques or a seasoned writer refining your craft, this book provides actionable guidance to help you unlock the full potential of your storytelling.

Practical Techniques

To effectively "show" rather than "tell," writers need a toolbox of techniques that can be applied across various aspects of storytelling. This book breaks down these techniques into manageable steps, ensuring clarity and applicability.

1. Using Sensory Details

- **What It Means:** Engage the reader's senses—sight, sound, touch, taste, and smell—to create vivid and memorable scenes.

- **Practical Tip:** Instead of saying, "The room was old and spooky," describe the creak of floorboards underfoot, the musty smell of forgotten belongings, and the flicker of a lone candle casting eerie shadows.

- **Why It Works:** Sensory details immerse readers in the scene, allowing them to feel as though they are part of the story.

2. Action Speaks Louder Than Words

- **What It Means:** Convey emotions and traits through actions rather than direct statements.

- **Practical Tip:** Show a character's anger by describing how they slam a door, clench their fists, or pace furiously, instead of writing, "He was angry."

- **Why It Works:** Actions are dynamic and engaging, allowing readers to infer emotions and motivations rather than being passively told about them.

3. Subtext in Dialogue

- **What It Means:** Use dialogue to reveal emotions, intentions, and relationships without being overly explicit.

- **Practical Tip:** Instead of having a character say, "I'm jealous of you," let their dialogue reflect their feelings indirectly: "Must be nice to always have things work out for you."

- **Why It Works:** Subtext adds layers to dialogue, making interactions feel authentic and intriguing.

4. Strategic Use of Setting

- **What It Means:** Let the environment reflect or amplify the mood and tone of a scene.

- **Practical Tip:** To show a character's loneliness, describe the vast emptiness of a beach at dawn, the waves crashing in a rhythmic but solitary cadence.

- **Why It Works:** Setting can act as an extension of a character's emotions, subtly reinforcing the story's themes.

5. Building Emotional Resonance

- **What It Means:** Use specific, relatable details to evoke emotion without melodrama.

- **Practical Tip:** Instead of stating, "She was heartbroken," show her carefully folding an old sweater she can no longer bear to wear, tears silently slipping down her cheeks.

- **Why It Works:** Readers connect deeply with tangible, specific moments that evoke universal emotions.

Examples and Exercises

This book provides a wealth of examples and exercises to reinforce the principles of "show, don't tell." These hands-on activities are designed to help writers put theory into practice, building confidence and skill.

Example 1: Transforming Telling Into Showing

- **Telling:** Emily was terrified of public speaking.

- **Showing:** Emily's palms slicked with sweat as she clutched the edges of the podium. Her voice wavered, barely audible over the pounding in her ears.

Exercise: Take the following sentences and rewrite them to show rather than tell:

- "Jacob was frustrated with his teammates."

- "The house was creepy."

- "Anna loved her dog."

Example 2: Creating Atmosphere Through Setting

- **Telling:** The forest was eerie and quiet.

- **Showing:** Twisted branches reached like skeletal fingers toward the dim sky. The crunch of dried leaves underfoot was the only sound, swallowed quickly by the heavy, oppressive silence.

Exercise: Write a paragraph describing an abandoned carnival using sensory details to evoke an unsettling atmosphere.

Example 3: Writing With Subtext

- **Telling:** Mark and Sarah were angry at each other but didn't want to argue in front of their kids.

- **Showing:** Mark's smile didn't reach his eyes as he handed Sarah the bowl of mashed potatoes. "More salt next time, maybe," he said lightly. Sarah's knuckles whitened as she gripped her fork, her gaze fixed on her plate. "Noted."

Exercise: Write a short dialogue between two characters who are hiding their true feelings during a formal dinner.

Example 4: Using Actions to Reveal Traits

- **Telling:** Alex was impatient.

- **Showing:** Alex tapped his foot against the tiled floor, his fingers drumming a rapid beat on the counter. He checked his watch twice in the span of a minute before exhaling sharply.

Exercise: Show a character's excitement without directly stating how they feel.

Guidance for All Levels of Writers

This book recognizes that writers come from diverse backgrounds and possess varying levels of experience. Its structure ensures that every reader, from beginners to advanced writers, can find value in the lessons provided.

For Beginners

- **Building a Strong Foundation:** The early chapters introduce the basics of "show, don't tell" in a clear and accessible manner, with straightforward examples and simple exercises.

- **Overcoming Common Challenges:** Practical advice addresses the fears and misconceptions that often hinder new writers, such as the fear of under-explaining or the tendency to overwrite.

- **Developing Confidence:** Exercises are designed to build skills gradually, fostering a sense of accomplishment with each completed task.

For Intermediate Writers

- **Refining Techniques:** Intermediate chapters delve deeper into advanced strategies, such as incorporating subtext and balancing showing with efficient storytelling.

- **Identifying Weak Spots:** Tips for self-editing and recognizing areas where telling might still creep into the prose help writers polish their work.

- **Expanding Versatility:** Exercises encourage experimentation with different genres and styles, broadening the writer's creative range.

For Advanced Writers

- **Mastering Subtlety:** Advanced sections focus on the nuances of showing, such as using symbolism and layering meaning within scenes.

- **Pushing Boundaries:** Challenging exercises inspire seasoned writers to push their creative limits, experimenting with unconventional techniques and perspectives.

- **Honing the Final Draft:** Practical advice for integrating feedback and perfecting the balance between showing and telling ensures that advanced writers can take their work to the next level.

Conclusion

This book is a comprehensive resource for mastering the art of "show, don't tell." By offering practical techniques, relatable examples, and engaging exercises, it empowers writers to create vivid, emotionally resonant stories that captivate readers. Whether you are just starting out or looking to refine your craft, the tools and insights provided in these pages will guide you toward becoming a more confident and effective storyteller. With dedication and practice, you can transform your writing, making every word count and every scene shine.

Chapter One

The Difference Between Showing and Telling

Understanding the difference between showing and telling is critical for writers seeking to craft immersive and emotionally engaging stories. While both techniques have their place in creative writing, showing is often the more effective approach for drawing readers into a story. In this section, we will define these terms, provide illustrative examples, and explore the emotional impact of showing versus telling.

Definitions and Examples

Telling involves directly conveying information to the reader in a straightforward manner. It relies on exposition to explain emotions, describe settings, or provide backstory. While clear and efficient, telling can often feel flat or disengaging because it removes the reader from the immediate experience of the story.

Showing, on the other hand, presents details through actions, dialogue, sensory descriptions, and subtext, allowing the reader to infer meaning. This approach invites readers to become active participants in the story by engaging their imagination and emotions.

Example 1: Describing a Character's Emotion

- **Telling:** Maria was angry.

- **Showing:** Maria's face turned crimson as she slammed the coffee mug onto the table, the sound echoing in the silent kitchen. "I can't believe you did that," she said, her voice trembling with barely contained fury.

In the telling example, the reader is simply informed of Maria's anger. In the showing example, the description of her actions, appearance, and dialogue allows the reader to infer her emotional state, creating a more vivid and engaging scene.

Example 2: Establishing Setting

- **Telling:** The forest was dark and spooky.

- **Showing:** The dense canopy of trees blocked out the moonlight, leaving the path ahead cloaked in shadows. Twigs snapped underfoot, and the air was heavy with the earthy scent of damp leaves. Somewhere in the distance, an owl hooted, its mournful call echoing through the stillness.

The telling example states the forest's atmosphere, but the showing example immerses the reader in the scene by using sensory details and specific imagery.

Example 3: Revealing a Character Trait

- **Telling:** James was generous.

- **Showing:** James reached into his pocket and pulled out a crumpled twenty-dollar bill. "Here," he said, handing it to the young boy. "Grab yourself something to eat. And keep the change."

By illustrating James' actions, the showing example demonstrates his generosity without explicitly stating it, allowing the reader to draw their own conclusions.

The Emotional Impact of Showing vs. Telling

The choice between showing and telling can significantly affect the emotional impact of a story. While telling provides information, showing creates an experience. Let's delve deeper into the emotional differences between the two approaches.

1. Engaging the Reader's Imagination

Telling often provides readers with the conclusion of an event or emotion without inviting them to engage with the details. For instance:

- **Telling:** The war was devastating for the town.

- **Showing:** Burned-out buildings lined the cobblestone streets, their roofs caved in like the hollowed shells of forgotten memories. Children with hollow eyes shuffled past, clutching scraps of bread as though their lives depended on them.

The showing example paints a vivid picture of the town's devastation, allowing readers to imagine and feel the consequences of the war. This engagement fosters a deeper emotional connection to the story.

2. Creating Emotional Resonance

Telling tends to describe emotions in a way that feels detached. Consider the following:

- **Telling:** She felt heartbroken.

- **Showing:** She traced the edges of the photograph with trembling fingers, her breath hitching as tears blurred the faces smiling back at her.

The showing example allows readers to experience the character's heartbreak through her actions and physical reactions, making the emotion feel more authentic and relatable.

3. Building Tension and Suspense

Showing is particularly effective for creating tension and suspense, as it reveals information gradually and leaves room for interpretation. For example:

- **Telling:** John was afraid of what was behind the door.

- **Showing:** John's hand hovered over the doorknob, his breath shallow and quick. The faint sound of scratching from the other side made him flinch, and his knees trembled as he stepped back.

By showing John's fear through his physical reactions and the atmosphere, the scene becomes more suspenseful and engaging, drawing readers into his experience.

4. Fostering Reader Investment

When writers tell, they provide readers with conclusions, leaving little room for personal interpretation or connection. In contrast, showing invites readers to piece together the story, fostering a sense of discovery and investment. For example:

- **Telling:** The protagonist was lonely.

- **Showing:** The empty apartment echoed with the sound of her footsteps. She sank into the worn armchair by the window, staring out at the bustling city below, her phone untouched on the table beside her.

In the showing example, readers can infer the protagonist's loneliness from the setting and her actions, making them more engaged in her experience.

5. Enhancing Character Development

Showing allows characters to reveal themselves through their actions, choices, and interactions, creating a more dynamic and layered portrayal. For example:

- **Telling:** Sarah was a hard worker.

- **Showing:** Sarah's alarm blared at 5 a.m., and she rolled out of bed without hesitation. By 7 a.m., she was at her desk, stacks of papers surrounding her, her pen moving steadily as the coffee in her mug grew cold.

The showing example provides specific actions that illustrate Sarah's dedication, allowing readers to understand her character more deeply.

6. Avoiding Clichés and Generic Writing

Telling often relies on clichés and generic phrases that fail to capture the uniqueness of a story. For instance:

- **Telling:** It was a beautiful sunset.

- **Showing:** Streaks of orange and pink stretched across the horizon, their brilliance reflected in the rippling waves. The sun dipped lower, casting a golden glow that seemed to set the world ablaze.

The showing example uses specific and vivid language to convey the beauty of the sunset, creating a more memorable and evocative image.

Balancing Showing and Telling

While showing is often more engaging, there are situations where telling is the better choice. For example:

1. **Efficiency:** Telling is useful for summarizing background information or transitions that do not require detailed exploration. For example:

    o   **Telling:** Over the next month, the team trained hard, improving their skills with each passing day.

2. **Pacing:** Telling can help maintain the flow of the narrative by avoiding unnecessary digressions. For instance:

    o   **Telling:** The storm passed quickly, leaving behind clear skies and a fresh breeze.

3. **Clarity:** Telling can clarify complex ideas or concepts that might be difficult to convey through showing alone. For example:

    o   **Telling:** He had spent years mastering the art of calligraphy, dedicating countless hours to perfecting each stroke.

The key is to find a balance between showing and telling that suits the story's needs. Showing should be used to create emotional depth and immerse readers in pivotal moments, while telling can be employed to provide context or move the narrative forward.

Conclusion

The difference between showing and telling lies in how information is conveyed to the reader. Telling provides straightforward explanations, while showing allows readers to experience the story through vivid details and actions. By understanding the emotional impact of these techniques and learning to balance them effectively, writers can create narratives that are both engaging and resonant. Mastering the art of showing is a powerful tool that brings stories to life, transforming readers from passive observers into active participants in the world of the story.

When To Show and When To Tell

The art of writing lies in knowing when to show and when to tell. While "showing" often creates a more engaging and immersive experience, "telling" has its place in keeping the story efficient and clear. The strategic use of both techniques allows writers to maintain pacing, provide essential information, and keep readers emotionally invested. In this section, we will explore how to balance these approaches and provide situational examples for their effective use.

Strategic Use of Both Techniques

Both showing and telling are essential tools in a writer's arsenal, each serving distinct purposes:

1. **Showing**

   o   Creates vivid and memorable scenes.

- o Engages readers emotionally by allowing them to infer meaning.

  - o Immerses readers in the narrative through sensory details and actions.

2. **Telling**

  - o Provides context and background information quickly.

  - o Summarizes events to maintain pacing.

  - o Clarifies complex concepts or transitions between scenes.

The key to using these techniques effectively is understanding their strengths and applying them where they serve the story best.

Situational Examples

1. Pacing

When to Show: Use showing to slow down and draw attention to significant moments. By adding rich details and sensory imagery, you can heighten the emotional impact of a scene.

Example:

- **Telling:** Sarah was nervous before her big performance.

- **Showing:** Sarah's hands trembled as she adjusted the microphone stand. The stage lights felt unbearably hot on her face, and her pulse thudded in her ears. She forced a smile, hoping it hid the butterflies wreaking havoc in her stomach.

By showing Sarah's nervousness, the reader experiences her emotions alongside her, creating a stronger connection.

When to Tell: Telling is useful for summarizing events or transitions that are not central to the plot, keeping the story's momentum.

Example:

- **Telling:** Over the next week, the team practiced tirelessly, reviewing their routines and perfecting every detail.

In this case, summarizing a week of practice helps maintain pacing while ensuring the reader knows the characters are preparing for an important event.

2. Transitions

When to Show: If the transition involves a pivotal moment or emotional shift, showing can deepen the reader's understanding of the characters and their journey.

Example:

- **Showing:** As the train pulled away, leaving behind the city she had called home for a decade, Clara stared out the window. The skyline faded into a blur, tears slipping down her cheeks as she clutched her suitcase tighter.

This transition emphasizes Clara's emotional state and the weight of her decision to leave.

When to Tell: For mundane or routine transitions, telling can move the story forward without unnecessary elaboration.

Example:

- **Telling:** The next morning, Clara arrived at her new apartment, ready to start fresh.

Summarizing the arrival keeps the narrative moving while setting the stage for the next scene.

3. Backstory

When to Show: When the backstory directly influences the plot or reveals a character's emotional state, showing can make the information more compelling.

Example:

- **Showing:** The faded photograph slipped from his pocket, revealing a younger version of himself standing next to a woman with a radiant smile. He traced her face with his thumb, his jaw tightening as he remembered the last time he had seen her.

This example conveys the significance of the woman through action and emotion, drawing the reader into the character's past.

When to Tell: For quick exposition or minor backstory details, telling ensures the reader has the necessary context without derailing the narrative.

Example:

- **Telling:** Ten years ago, he had left the woman he loved to pursue a career overseas, a decision that still haunted him.

Here, the information is presented succinctly, keeping the focus on the present storyline.

4. Developing Characters

When to Show: Use showing to reveal a character's personality, emotions, or growth through actions and interactions.

Example:

- **Showing:** Emily picked up the stray puppy, her hands trembling as she wrapped it in her scarf. "We'll find you a home," she whispered, brushing away a tear.

This example demonstrates Emily's compassion without explicitly stating it, allowing readers to infer her traits.

When to Tell: Telling can be helpful for introducing minor characters or summarizing traits that are not central to the story.

Example:

- **Telling:** Emily had always been kind-hearted, often putting others' needs before her own.

This concise description provides context without diverting focus from the main narrative.

5. Creating Atmosphere

When to Show: Use showing to build atmosphere and immerse readers in the setting.

Example:

- **Showing:** The storm raged outside, rain lashing against the windows and wind howling through the cracks in the old cabin's walls. The flickering candlelight cast long, shifting shadows across the room.

This example uses sensory details to create a vivid, immersive atmosphere.

When to Tell: Telling can efficiently establish setting when the details are not central to the scene.

Example:

- **Telling:** It was a dark and stormy night, with rain pounding relentlessly against the cabin.

While less immersive, this summary provides enough context to set the scene quickly.

6. Highlighting Themes

When to Show: Showing allows readers to uncover themes organically through characters' experiences and choices.

Example:

- **Showing:** As she watched the young boy share his sandwich with a stray dog, Maria felt a pang of guilt. She had ignored the beggar outside the café just an hour earlier, her own sandwich untouched on the table.

This scene subtly introduces themes of compassion and guilt, letting readers infer the message.

When to Tell: Telling can underscore themes explicitly, especially in moments of reflection or conclusion.

Example:

- **Telling:** Maria realized she had been too focused on herself, missing opportunities to help those in need.

This direct statement reinforces the theme but lacks the emotional depth of the showing example.

Tips for Balancing Showing and Telling

1. **Consider the Importance of the Scene:** Reserve showing for moments that are emotionally significant or pivotal to the plot. Use telling for less critical information.

2. **Blend Techniques:** Combine showing and telling within a scene to maintain clarity while creating depth. For example:

   - **Blended Example:** Over the next week, the team practiced tirelessly, reviewing their routines and perfecting every detail. By the final rehearsal, their synchronized movements and confident smiles showed just how far they had come.

3. **Read Aloud:** Hearing your writing can help identify whether a section feels too expository or overly detailed.

4. **Get Feedback:** Beta readers can highlight areas where more showing or telling might improve the narrative.

Conclusion

Knowing when to show and when to tell is a skill that requires practice and discernment. Showing immerses readers in the story and evokes emotional connections, while telling provides clarity and efficiency. By strategically using both techniques and understanding their situational applications, writers can craft stories that are both engaging and well-paced. Balancing showing and telling ensures that each moment of your narrative resonates with readers, drawing them deeper into the world you have created.

The Role of the Reader

Writers craft stories with the intention of engaging their audience, but a vital part of the storytelling process lies in the hands of the reader. Readers are not passive recipients of information; they are active participants who interpret, imagine, and connect with the narrative. Understanding the role of the reader is essential for writers aiming to create meaningful and immersive experiences. In this section, we will explore how to engage readers' imaginations and build trust with the audience, ensuring that the relationship between writer and reader enhances the story.

Engaging Readers' Imaginations

One of the most powerful aspects of storytelling is its ability to ignite the imagination. When writers show rather than tell, they invite readers to visualize scenes, empathize with characters, and infer underlying emotions and themes. This collaborative process transforms reading from a passive activity into an active and personal experience.

1. Providing Just Enough Detail

Engaging the reader's imagination begins with providing enough detail to paint a vivid picture while leaving room for interpretation. Over-explaining or describing every aspect of a scene can stifle creativity, whereas carefully chosen details allow readers to fill in the gaps with their own mental images.

Example:

- **Over-explaining:** The dining room table was rectangular, made of polished mahogany, with six matching chairs upholstered in beige fabric. A vase of red roses sat in the center, surrounded by neatly arranged silverware.

- **Engaging:** A polished mahogany table gleamed under the soft glow of the chandelier, its centerpiece a vase of fresh red roses.

The second example provides key details but leaves enough space for readers to imagine the rest of the scene, fostering a more engaging experience.

2. Using Sensory Language

Sensory language is a powerful tool for activating the reader's imagination. Describing how something looks, sounds, feels, smells, or tastes allows readers to immerse themselves in the story and create a mental representation of the world.

Example:

- Instead of saying, "The bakery smelled nice," write, "The scent of freshly baked bread and sweet cinnamon rolls wafted through the air, wrapping around her like a warm embrace."

By appealing to the senses, writers can evoke vivid imagery and emotional responses, drawing readers deeper into the narrative.

3. Encouraging Inference

Part of engaging readers' imaginations involves encouraging them to infer meaning rather than presenting everything explicitly. Subtext, symbolism, and subtle cues invite readers to uncover layers of the story on their own, creating a sense of discovery.

Example:

- **Explicit:** John was jealous of his coworker's promotion.

- **Subtle:** John's smile faltered as he clapped along with the others, his fingers tightening around the glass in his hand.

The second example encourages readers to interpret John's emotions through his actions, making the scene more engaging and thought-provoking.

4. Creating Relatable Characters

Relatable characters are key to capturing readers' imaginations. When readers see aspects of themselves or people they know in the characters, they are more likely to invest emotionally in the story.

Techniques:

- Show characters facing universal struggles, such as self-doubt, love, loss, or ambition.

- Highlight quirks and imperfections to make characters feel authentic.

- Allow characters to grow and change over the course of the narrative, mirroring the complexities of real life.

5. Leaving Room for Interpretation

Not every question in a story needs to be answered
outright. Leaving certain elements open to interpretation
can spark discussions and allow readers to bring their own
perspectives to the narrative.

Example:

- At the end of a mystery, instead of revealing every
  detail, leave a few clues unresolved, letting readers
  theorize about what really happened.

This approach engages the reader beyond the final page,
keeping the story alive in their minds.

Building Trust with the Audience

The relationship between writer and reader is built on trust.
Readers trust writers to provide a coherent and satisfying
story, while writers trust readers to engage with the material
thoughtfully. Establishing and maintaining this trust is
crucial for a successful storytelling experience.

1. Consistency in Narrative

Readers need to feel that the world of the story operates
within a consistent set of rules. Whether the story is set in a
realistic or fantastical world, maintaining internal logic
ensures that readers remain immersed.

Example:

- If a character in a fantasy novel suddenly discovers
  a new magical ability, there should be groundwork
  laid earlier in the story to make this development
  believable.

Consistency builds trust by showing that the writer respects the reader's intelligence and attention to detail.

2. Authenticity in Emotion

Readers can sense when emotions in a story feel forced or contrived. Authentic emotional moments resonate because they reflect genuine human experiences.

Techniques:

- Draw from real-life observations or personal experiences to create believable emotional arcs.

- Avoid clichés and melodrama, opting for subtle and nuanced expressions of emotion.

Example:

- Instead of having a character scream, "I'm heartbroken!" show them sitting quietly in a dark room, staring at an untouched cup of coffee.

3. Avoiding Over-Exposition

Overloading readers with information can make a story feel didactic or patronizing. Trust readers to piece together the story from context and subtext.

Example:

- Instead of describing every detail of a character's backstory in a single paragraph, reveal it gradually through dialogue, flashbacks, or interactions with other characters.

By trusting readers to connect the dots, writers create a more dynamic and engaging narrative.

4. Delivering on Promises

When a writer sets up expectations, whether through foreshadowing, themes, or plot threads, it is important to follow through. Failing to address major questions or resolve key conflicts can leave readers feeling frustrated or betrayed.

Example:

- If a story introduces a mysterious locked chest in the first chapter, ensure that its contents are revealed or its purpose explained by the end.

Fulfilled promises reinforce the reader's trust in the writer and make the story more satisfying.

5. Acknowledging Reader Intelligence

Respecting the reader's ability to understand and interpret the story is crucial for building trust. Avoid over-explaining or simplifying complex ideas.

Example:

- Instead of writing, "This symbolizes the character's freedom," show the character opening a cage and watching a bird take flight. Trust readers to grasp the metaphor without spelling it out.

By giving readers the space to think and engage critically, writers show respect for their audience, strengthening the connection between them.

6. Balancing Mystery and Clarity

While it is important to maintain a sense of mystery and intrigue, ensuring that essential aspects of the story are clear prevents confusion and frustration.

Example:

- A thriller can leave the identity of the villain uncertain until the climax, but the motivations and stakes should be clearly established to keep readers invested.

Balancing these elements keeps readers intrigued without alienating them.

Conclusion

The role of the reader in storytelling is both active and essential. By engaging readers' imaginations, writers can create vivid and memorable narratives that resonate on a personal level. Building trust with the audience ensures that the story remains coherent, emotionally authentic, and satisfying. When writers embrace the reader's role as a collaborator in the storytelling process, they open the door to deeper connections and more impactful stories. Balancing these elements is the key to crafting narratives that not only captivate but also endure in the minds and hearts of readers.

Chapter Two

Writing with the Five Senses

Using the five senses—sight, sound, touch, taste, and smell—is one of the most effective ways to bring a story to life. Sensory details create vivid imagery, immerse readers in the narrative, and evoke emotions by engaging their imagination. Mastering this technique requires understanding how to incorporate sensory language effectively and avoiding the pitfalls of sensory overload.

How to Incorporate the Five Senses

Each sense adds a unique layer of depth and realism to a story. By using sensory details selectively and purposefully, writers can enhance their storytelling without overwhelming the reader.

1. Sight: The Visual World

Sight is the most commonly used sense in writing, as readers naturally visualize the scenes described. Effective visual descriptions go beyond the obvious to highlight details that evoke mood, reveal character, or set the tone.

Examples:

- **Basic Sight Description:** The garden was full of flowers.

- **Enhanced Sight Description:** Petals of crimson and gold swayed in the breeze, their colors vibrant against the soft green of the moss-covered path.

Techniques for Incorporating Sight:

- Use contrasts: Light and shadow, color and monotone, clarity and obscurity.

- Focus on unique or unusual details: A chipped teacup, a single wilted flower among a thriving bed.

- Avoid laundry lists: Instead of cataloging every element of a scene, pick a few striking details to focus on.

2. Sound: The Invisible Symphony

Sound adds dimension and atmosphere, whether it's the murmur of voices in a crowded café or the eerie creak of a door in a haunted house. Sounds can also reveal action and contribute to tension or calm.

Examples:

- **Basic Sound Description:** The city was noisy.

- **Enhanced Sound Description:** Car horns blared in the distance, mingling with the rhythmic clatter of subway trains and the occasional bark of a street vendor advertising his wares.

Techniques for Incorporating Sound:

- Use onomatopoeia: Words that imitate sounds (e.g., "sizzle," "crack") can bring scenes to life.

- Layer sounds: Describe how multiple noises interact or contrast.

- Highlight silence: The absence of sound can be just as powerful as noise, creating tension or emphasizing solitude.

3. Touch: The Texture of Experience

Describing touch helps readers feel the physical world of your story. This can range from the texture of objects to the sensation of temperature, pressure, or pain.

Examples:

- **Basic Touch Description:** The fabric was soft.

- **Enhanced Touch Description:** Her fingers brushed against the velvet, its surface cool and smooth, with a hint of resistance as she pressed down.

Techniques for Incorporating Touch:

- Use adjectives sparingly: Choose precise words to describe textures (e.g., "slick," "grainy").

- Describe sensations: Heat, cold, wetness, dryness, or the prick of a thorn.

- Highlight emotional connections: A rough calloused hand might suggest hard labor; a soft blanket might evoke comfort or nostalgia.

4. Taste: Flavoring the Narrative

Taste is a less frequently used sense but can be incredibly impactful when tied to specific moments. It's particularly useful in scenes involving food, drink, or environments where taste adds to the sensory experience (e.g., salt in the air near the ocean).

Examples:

- **Basic Taste Description:** The soup was delicious.

- **Enhanced Taste Description:** The soup was rich and savory, with a tangy hint of lemon that lingered on her tongue long after the last spoonful.

Techniques for Incorporating Taste:

- Connect taste to memory: A particular flavor can evoke a past experience or emotion.

- Be specific: Use terms that describe flavor profiles (e.g., "sour," "spicy," "smoky").

- Integrate other senses: Combine taste with smell or texture to create a fuller picture (e.g., "the creamy chocolate melted on her tongue, its sweetness mingling with the faint bitterness of roasted cacao").

5. Smell: The Lingering Memory

Smell is one of the most evocative senses, closely linked to memory and emotion. A single scent can transport characters—and readers—to another time or place.

Examples:

- **Basic Smell Description:** The flowers smelled nice.

- **Enhanced Smell Description:** The roses exuded a heady, honeyed aroma that mingled with the earthy tang of freshly turned soil.

Techniques for Incorporating Smell:

- Tie smells to emotions: The scent of fresh bread might evoke comfort; the smell of smoke might trigger fear.

- Be specific: Use descriptors that convey intensity and character (e.g., "musky," "pungent," "faint").

- Layer scents: Describe how multiple odors interact, such as the mingling of perfume, sweat, and spilled wine at a party.

Avoiding Sensory Overload

While sensory details enrich a story, overloading the reader with too many at once can be counterproductive. Too much description can slow pacing, distract from the narrative, and overwhelm the reader's imagination. Here are strategies for balancing sensory language effectively:

1. Prioritize Key Details

Focus on the most important sensory elements that advance the plot, reveal character, or establish mood. Avoid the temptation to describe everything in a scene.

Example:

- Instead of: "The room smelled of lavender, lemon, and old books, and the walls were painted a soft cream, with sunlight streaming through lace curtains onto the wooden floor, which creaked slightly as she stepped, her shoes scuffing against the surface."

- Write: "The scent of lavender mingled with the musty aroma of old books as sunlight streamed through lace curtains, highlighting the creaking wooden floor."

2. Integrate Sensory Details Naturally

Weave sensory descriptions into the action and dialogue rather than isolating them in blocks of text.

Example:

- Instead of: "The coffee was bitter and hot. The room was quiet, except for the ticking clock. The table felt smooth beneath her fingers."

- Write: "She sipped her coffee, its bitter heat making her wince. The only sound was the steady tick of the clock as her fingers traced the smooth surface of the table."

3. Match the Tone and Pacing

Adapt sensory descriptions to fit the mood and rhythm of the scene. In fast-paced action scenes, brief sensory impressions work better than lengthy descriptions. In slower, introspective moments, more detailed sensory language can deepen the reader's immersion.

Example:

- Fast-paced: "Gunpowder burned her nose as shouts and screams filled the air."

- Slow-paced: "The delicate scent of lilacs lingered in the air, a reminder of spring mornings spent wandering through the garden."

4. Avoid Repetition

Repeating the same type of sensory detail can become monotonous. Vary the senses you focus on to create a well-rounded experience.

Example:

- Instead of describing how every object in a room looks, include sounds, smells, and textures to add variety.

5. Use Restraint

Sometimes less is more. A single, well-chosen sensory detail can be more impactful than an exhaustive description.

Example:

- Instead of: "The wind was cold and sharp, biting at her cheeks and stinging her eyes. The snow was wet and heavy, soaking through her boots. Her scarf was scratchy against her skin."

- Write: "The icy wind stung her cheeks as heavy snow soaked through her boots."

Conclusion

Incorporating the five senses into your writing can transform your storytelling, making it more vivid, immersive, and emotionally resonant. By focusing on sight, sound, touch, taste, and smell, you can bring your scenes to life and create a richer experience for your readers. Remember to balance sensory details with narrative pacing and to use them purposefully to enhance the story. With practice, you'll master the art of engaging your readers' senses, drawing them fully into the worlds you create.

Using Metaphors and Similes

Metaphors and similes are indispensable tools in creative writing, enabling writers to create vivid imagery and convey complex ideas in accessible ways. These figurative devices enrich the narrative by drawing connections between the familiar and the unfamiliar, allowing readers to visualize and emotionally connect with the story. However, using metaphors and similes effectively requires balancing creativity with clarity to avoid confusion or overloading the prose.

Creating Vivid Imagery

The primary function of metaphors and similes is to make abstract concepts or ordinary descriptions more vivid and memorable. By comparing one thing to another, these devices evoke sensory responses, deepen emotional resonance, and enhance the reader's experience.

1. Crafting Original Comparisons

Original metaphors and similes captivate readers and breathe fresh life into your writing. Avoid clichés like "busy as a bee" or "cold as ice," which have lost their impact through overuse. Instead, strive for unique and specific comparisons that align with the tone and context of your story.

Example:

- **Cliché:** Her smile was as bright as the sun.

- **Original:** Her smile lit the room like the first break of dawn after a storm.

By using a specific and vivid image, the second example conveys warmth and hope, making it more impactful.

2. Appealing to the Senses

Metaphors and similes are particularly effective when they engage the reader's senses. A well-crafted comparison can help readers see, hear, smell, taste, or feel what the character is experiencing.

Example:

- **Sight:** The city lights spread across the horizon like scattered stars on a velvet canvas.

- **Sound:** His voice was a deep rumble, like distant thunder rolling across the plains.

- **Smell:** The air was thick with the smell of gasoline, sharp and acrid like a struck match.

3. Revealing Character and Emotion

Figurative language can also reveal a character's personality, emotions, or worldview. The comparisons they make might reflect their background, mood, or state of mind.

Example:

- A jaded detective might describe the city as "a beast that never sleeps, its neon eyes glaring down on the streets."

- A romantic character might see the same city as "a glittering jewel, alive with endless possibilities."

By tailoring metaphors and similes to a character's perspective, you deepen their portrayal and enrich the narrative voice.

4. Enhancing Mood and Tone

Metaphors and similes can set the mood and tone of a scene, shaping how readers feel as they progress through the story. The imagery you choose should align with the atmosphere you want to create.

Examples:

- To create a sense of foreboding: "The trees stood like sentinels, their gnarled branches clawing at the sky."

- To evoke tranquility: "The lake shimmered like a sheet of glass, undisturbed by the gentle whispers of the breeze."

Balancing Creativity with Clarity

While metaphors and similes can elevate writing, using them excessively or inappropriately can confuse readers or disrupt the flow of the narrative. Striking a balance between creativity and clarity is essential.

1. Avoid Overloading the Prose

Too many metaphors and similes in close proximity can overwhelm the reader and dilute their impact. Instead, use them sparingly and strategically to emphasize key moments or ideas.

Example of Overuse:

- "Her hair was as golden as the sun, cascading like a waterfall over her shoulders. Her eyes sparkled like diamonds, and her voice was like a melody carried on the wind."

Revised:

- "Her golden hair cascaded over her shoulders, her voice carrying the softness of a melody."

The revised version retains vivid imagery without becoming overly flowery or repetitive.

2. Ensure the Comparison Fits the Context

Metaphors and similes should feel natural within the story's context. A poorly chosen or forced comparison can confuse readers or pull them out of the narrative.

Example of Misfit:

- In a gritty crime novel: "The blood pooled on the floor like strawberry syrup."

Revised:

- "The blood pooled on the floor, dark and viscous like spilled ink."

The second example maintains the tone of the story and avoids an inappropriate or jarring image.

3. Avoid Mixing Metaphors

Mixed metaphors occur when two incompatible comparisons are combined, leading to confusion or unintentional humor.

Example of a Mixed Metaphor:

- "We need to get all our ducks in a row before the ship sails."

Revised:

- Choose one: "We need to get all our ducks in a row" or "We need to prepare before the ship sails."

Keeping comparisons consistent ensures that the imagery is clear and effective.

4. Use Simple and Accessible Language

While it's tempting to craft elaborate or obscure metaphors, clarity should always take precedence. Readers should be able to understand the comparison without effort.

Example of Complexity:

- "Her laughter rippled through the room like the elusive harmonics of a Stradivarius, delicate yet resonant in its complexity."

Revised:

- "Her laughter rippled through the room, light and melodious like a gentle breeze."

The revised version is more straightforward while still being evocative.

5. Test for Longevity

Consider whether the metaphor or simile will stand the test of time. Comparisons that rely on fleeting trends or obscure references may lose their impact over the years.

Example of a Trend-Based Metaphor:

- "His words hit her like a viral meme, spreading shock and laughter."

Revised:

- "His words hit her like a sudden gust of wind, leaving her off balance."

The revised version uses a timeless image that will resonate with a broader audience.

Exercises for Practicing Metaphors and Similes

1. **Transform the Ordinary:** Take a simple sentence and rewrite it using a metaphor or simile. For example:

   o   Ordinary: "The room was very quiet."

   o   With a Simile: "The room was as quiet as a church at midnight."

2. **Character Perspective:** Write a metaphor or simile from the perspective of a specific character. For instance:

   o   A child might describe a thunderstorm as "clouds having an angry argument," while a scientist might see it as "Nature's electrical orchestra."

3. **Thematic Imagery:** Create three metaphors or similes that align with a central theme in your story. For example, if your theme is resilience, you might write:

   o   "She stood firm, like a lighthouse battered by endless waves."

4. **Streamlining Overwritten Comparisons:** Take an overwritten paragraph filled with metaphors and similes, and condense it into a more focused and impactful version.

5. **Identify and Revise Clichés:** List common clichés and rewrite them with fresh, original imagery. For example:

   o Cliché: "He was as strong as an ox."

   o Revised: "He was as unyielding as a granite cliff."

Conclusion

Metaphors and similes are powerful tools for creating vivid imagery and deepening the reader's connection to the story. By crafting original and context-appropriate comparisons, appealing to the senses, and balancing creativity with clarity, writers can elevate their prose and leave a lasting impression. With practice and careful application, these devices can transform ordinary descriptions into extraordinary moments, enriching the narrative and engaging the reader on a profound level.

Examples and Exercises: Practice Writing Scenes with Strong Sensory Detail

Strong sensory details transform ordinary writing into an immersive experience, drawing readers into the world of the story. The following examples and exercises are designed to help you develop and refine your ability to incorporate sensory language effectively.

Example 1: A Rainy Street

- **Without Sensory Detail:** "The street was wet after the rain."

- **With Sensory Detail:** "The street glistened under the dim glow of the streetlights, each puddle shimmering like molten silver. The air was thick with the smell of damp asphalt and rain-soaked leaves. A distant car splashed through a puddle, its tires hissing against the slick pavement."

This revision uses sight ("glistened," "molten silver"), sound ("hissing tires"), and smell ("damp asphalt and rain-soaked leaves") to paint a vivid picture.

Exercise 1: Write a scene set in a forest just after a storm. Use at least three senses (sight, sound, and smell) to create a vivid image.

Example 2: A Crowded Marketplace

- **Without Sensory Detail:** "The marketplace was busy and loud."

- **With Sensory Detail:** "Vendors shouted over one another, their voices blending into a chaotic symphony of bartering and laughter. The scent of ripe mangoes mingled with the sharp tang of spices, while the heat of the midday sun pressed down, making every breath feel heavy. Brightly colored fabrics fluttered in the breeze, catching the sunlight like jewels."

This version engages sight ("brightly colored fabrics"), sound ("chaotic symphony"), smell ("ripe mangoes," "tang of spices"), and touch ("heat of the midday sun").

Exercise 2: Describe a bustling café. Focus on the sounds (e.g., clinking cups, murmured conversations) and smells (e.g., fresh coffee, baked goods). Avoid using generic terms like "busy" or "loud."

Example 3: A Haunted House

- **Without Sensory Detail:** "The house felt scary."

- **With Sensory Detail:** "The wooden floorboards groaned with every step, and a cold draft slithered through the cracks in the walls, carrying with it the faint, musty scent of mildew. Cobwebs clung to the corners of the ceiling, shimmering faintly in the moonlight that seeped through a broken window. Somewhere deep within the house, a door creaked, its sound sharp and sudden like a cry in the silence."

Here, sensory details evoke the eerie atmosphere, engaging sight ("cobwebs," "moonlight"), sound ("groaned," "creaked"), and touch ("cold draft").

Exercise 3: Write a description of an abandoned playground at dusk. Incorporate sounds (e.g., creaking swings), sights (e.g., rusted play structures), and touch (e.g., the chill of the evening air).

Example 4: A Family Dinner

- **Without Sensory Detail:** "The dinner was nice and everyone seemed happy."

- **With Sensory Detail:** "The table was crowded with steaming dishes: roasted chicken glistening with juices, buttery mashed potatoes, and warm rolls whose aroma filled the air. Glasses clinked as laughter erupted from one end of the table, a light, joyous sound that mingled with the occasional scrape of utensils on plates. The warmth of the kitchen seemed to wrap around everyone, a comforting cocoon against the chill outside."

This revision uses sight ("steaming dishes"), sound ("laughter," "glasses clinked"), smell ("aroma of warm rolls"), and touch ("warmth of the kitchen").

Exercise 4: Write a scene where a character is enjoying a favorite meal at a small diner. Include sensory details to capture the setting, the food, and the character's emotions.

Tips for Practicing Sensory Writing

1. **Focus on One Sense at a Time:** Start by describing a scene using only one sense, such as sound or smell. Once you're comfortable, layer in other senses.

2. **Show, Don't Tell:** Use sensory details to evoke emotions or set the mood without explicitly stating how the character feels. For instance, instead of saying, "She felt nervous," describe her sweaty palms or the way her pulse pounded in her ears.

3. **Be Specific:** Avoid generic descriptions. Instead of saying, "The flowers smelled nice," describe the

specific scent: "The roses exuded a heady, honeyed aroma."

4. **Balance Details:** While sensory language is powerful, too much can overwhelm the reader. Focus on the most impactful details and let the reader fill in the gaps.

By practicing these exercises and techniques, you'll develop the ability to create immersive, sensory-rich scenes that captivate your readers.

Chapter Three

Creating Immersive Characters

Showing Character Traits

Revealing character traits is a fundamental aspect of storytelling, helping readers understand and connect with the individuals in your narrative. While it's tempting to list a character's qualities directly, this approach often results in static and disengaging prose. Instead, showing character traits through actions, dialogue, and decisions allows readers to experience the character's personality dynamically. This approach deepens engagement, builds complexity, and avoids the dreaded "info dump" that can stall the momentum of a story.

Revealing Personality Through Actions

Actions are one of the most effective ways to demonstrate a character's personality. What a character does—or chooses not to do—can speak volumes about their values, fears, and desires.

1. Everyday Actions

Characters' day-to-day behaviors can subtly reveal who they are. For instance, a character who meticulously organizes their desk every morning might value order and control, while another who leaves coffee cups and scattered papers behind may prioritize creativity over tidiness.

Example:

- **Orderly Character:** "She straightened the picture frame on her desk, aligning it perfectly with the edge. The stack of papers beside her was organized by size, each sheet squared to the corner."

- **Messy Character:** "He tossed another coffee-stained napkin onto the heap, its crumpled surface collapsing into the chaos of scattered notebooks and loose pens."

These small details provide insight into each character's personality without overt explanation.

2. Reactions to Conflict

How a character reacts under pressure reveals much about their core traits. A compassionate character might step in to help someone in danger, while a cautious one might hesitate or retreat.

Example:

- **Compassionate Reaction:** "As the cyclist tumbled onto the pavement, she dropped her groceries and ran to his side, ignoring the apples rolling into the gutter."

- **Cautious Reaction:** "She froze as the cyclist fell, her hand tightening on the strap of her purse. After a long moment, she crossed to the other side of the street, her gaze fixed firmly ahead."

By illustrating how characters behave in challenging situations, you show their personalities in action.

3. Unique Mannerisms

Quirks and habits can make characters memorable while also hinting at their inner lives. A character who constantly checks their watch might be anxious or time-conscious, while one who doodles during meetings might have a creative or inattentive streak.

Example:

- "He tapped his pen rhythmically against the table, the clicking sound quickening whenever the conversation shifted toward him."

These details help define characters in a way that feels organic and engaging.

Revealing Personality Through Dialogue

Dialogue is a powerful tool for showing character traits. The way characters speak, what they choose to say, and how they interact with others reveal their personalities and relationships.

1. Word Choice and Tone

Characters' vocabulary, tone, and manner of speaking can reflect their background, education, and temperament.

Example:

- **Formal Character:** "I must insist that we adhere to the schedule. Delays are simply unacceptable."

- **Casual Character:** "Eh, we'll get there when we get there. No big deal."

By tailoring dialogue to each character, you bring their unique voice to life.

2. Subtext and Hidden Meanings

Subtext in dialogue reveals what a character is feeling or thinking without stating it outright. This indirect approach can highlight traits like sarcasm, vulnerability, or cunning.

Example:

- "Oh, of course, you'd know all about that," she said with a thin smile, her tone as sharp as the edge of a blade.

Here, the character's sarcasm hints at underlying resentment, showing more than the surface words convey.

3. Interactions with Others

How characters speak to others—whether with kindness, condescension, or indifference—can show their values and social dynamics.

Example:

- **Kind Character:** "Don't worry about it," he said, crouching to pick up the scattered papers. "Happens to the best of us."

- **Abrasive Character:** "Seriously? Watch where you're going next time," he snapped, brushing past without a second glance.

Through dialogue, you can reveal relationships and social dynamics while deepening characterization.

Revealing Personality Through Decisions

A character's choices, particularly in moments of conflict or moral ambiguity, are among the most revealing aspects of their personality. Decisions showcase priorities, values, and flaws.

1. Moral Dilemmas

Placing characters in situations where they must make difficult choices reveals their ethical compass. A character's decision to save a friend at great personal risk, for example, might show loyalty and bravery, while another's choice to prioritize self-preservation could indicate pragmatism or fear.

Example:

- "The fire roared higher, licking at the beams overhead. She glanced at the photo on the mantelpiece, then at the door. A second later, she was running, the photograph clutched tightly in her hand."

This choice highlights the character's priorities and emotional attachments.

2. Small, Everyday Decisions

Even seemingly mundane decisions can reveal character traits. Choosing to take the scenic route home might suggest a contemplative or adventurous nature, while opting for the quickest path could indicate efficiency or impatience.

Example:

- "When the barista handed her the wrong drink, she hesitated, then smiled and took a sip. She didn't want to make a fuss."

This small decision shows the character's inclination to avoid conflict and her easygoing nature.

3. Long-Term Goals and Plans

Characters' aspirations and the steps they take to achieve them demonstrate ambition, perseverance, or recklessness.

Example:

- "He stayed up late every night, poring over diagrams and calculations. If he could just perfect the design, the grant money might finally come through."

This determination and dedication reveal the character's work ethic and hope for the future.

Avoiding Character "Info Dumps"

One of the biggest pitfalls in character development is the "info dump"—an expository passage that tells the reader everything about a character at once. This approach can feel unnatural and detract from the story's flow.

1. Integrate Information Gradually

Rather than presenting all of a character's traits at once, reveal them over time through their actions, dialogue, and decisions.

Example of an Info Dump:

- "James was a 35-year-old engineer who loved hiking and cooking. He was detail-oriented but often struggled with indecision."

Revised:

- "James adjusted the blueprint for the third time, frowning at the uneven lines. He reached for his coffee, now cold, and sighed. Maybe a hike this weekend would help him clear his head."

The revised version shows James's traits through his actions and thoughts, weaving them naturally into the scene.

2. Show Traits Through Relationships

Reveal character traits through their interactions with others. A character's behavior toward friends, family, or strangers can provide insight without overt explanation.

Example:

- "When her sister showed up unexpectedly, Maria's irritation vanished. She pulled her inside, laughing as she grabbed a pair of slippers from the closet."

This moment demonstrates Maria's warmth and adaptability without explicitly stating those qualities.

3. Use Conflict and Change

Conflict pushes characters to reveal their true selves, while change shows growth over time. By embedding traits within the plot, you make them integral to the story.

Example:

- "At first, Liam avoided the volunteer sign-up sheet. But after seeing the kids playing soccer with patched-up balls, he scribbled his name in the last slot."

This arc reveals Liam's initial reluctance and eventual compassion, showing his growth through action.

Conclusion

Showing character traits through actions, dialogue, and decisions creates dynamic, engaging storytelling. By avoiding info dumps and weaving traits naturally into the narrative, writers can craft characters who feel authentic and relatable. Practice these techniques to reveal your characters' personalities in ways that draw readers deeper into your story and leave a lasting impression.

Subtext In Dialog

Subtext in dialogue refers to the unspoken or implied meaning beneath the surface of a conversation. Rather than directly stating emotions or intentions, subtext allows readers to infer what characters are truly feeling or thinking based on what they say, how they say it, and what they leave unsaid. This technique adds depth and realism to dialogue, making interactions more engaging and authentic. Mastering subtext requires an understanding of human behavior, emotional nuance, and subtlety in language.

Conveying Emotions and Intentions Without Explicit Statements

Directly stating emotions or intentions in dialogue can feel unnatural or overly simplistic. Instead, subtext creates a layer of complexity that mirrors real-life conversations, where people often conceal their true feelings or communicate indirectly.

1. Using Body Language and Tone

Subtext often emerges through non-verbal cues that accompany dialogue. Characters may say one thing while their body language, tone, or actions suggest something entirely different.

Example:

- **Explicit:** "I'm angry with you for being late."

- **With Subtext:** "Oh, you made it. I was starting to think the clock stopped working," she said, crossing her arms and tapping her foot.

In the second example, the character's sarcasm and body language convey her anger without explicitly stating it. Readers can infer her feelings through context.

2. Contradictions Between Words and Actions

When a character's words contradict their actions, it creates subtext that reveals their true feelings or intentions.

Example:

- Dialogue: "I'm fine, really."

- Action: The character avoids eye contact, their hands trembling as they reach for their drink.

The subtext suggests that the character is not fine, despite their words.

3. Pauses and Hesitation

Hesitation, unfinished sentences, or pauses can indicate discomfort, uncertainty, or hidden intentions.

Example:

- Dialogue: "I thought we could maybe… never mind. It's stupid."

Here, the ellipsis and abrupt dismissal of the thought imply vulnerability or fear of rejection.

4. Understated Responses

Sometimes, what a character doesn't say is as telling as what they do say. Understated responses can convey reluctance, resentment, or emotional restraint.

Example:

- Character A: "Are you upset with me?"

- Character B: "Why would I be?" (delivered with a tight smile).

The subtext here suggests that Character B is upset but unwilling to admit it outright.

5. Context and Situation

The context in which dialogue occurs can create subtext. A seemingly innocent statement can carry a different meaning depending on the situation.

Example:

- At a tense dinner party, a character says, "Well, isn't this cozy?"

Depending on the tone and context, this could imply sarcasm, discomfort, or genuine warmth.

Techniques for Writing Layered Conversations

Creating dialogue with subtext requires a careful balance of what is said, unsaid, and implied. The following techniques can help writers craft layered and meaningful conversations.

1. Imply, Don't State

Leave room for the reader to interpret the underlying meaning of a conversation. Avoid explaining the subtext outright; instead, trust readers to pick up on subtle cues.

Example:

- **Explicit:** "I feel like you're trying to control me."

- **With Subtext:** "You always have a suggestion for how I should do things, don't you?"

The second example implies control without explicitly stating it, encouraging readers to infer the tension.

2. Use Metaphors and Indirect References

Characters can use metaphors, anecdotes, or indirect references to convey their emotions or intentions without addressing them directly.

Example:

- Dialogue: "You know, sharks keep swimming or they'll die. Sometimes I feel like I'm stuck doing the same thing."

The metaphor suggests the character's feelings of exhaustion or entrapment without directly stating it.

3. Layer Conflicting Motivations

Characters often have multiple motivations that influence their dialogue. Highlighting these conflicts can create rich subtext.

Example:

- A character wants to express affection but fears vulnerability: "I guess it's nice having someone around who doesn't drive me completely insane."

The subtext reveals affection disguised as teasing, hinting at the character's fear of being too direct.

4. Establish Power Dynamics

Subtext can highlight power dynamics between characters. A subordinate character might phrase their disagreement cautiously, while a dominant character might mask manipulation as concern.

Example:

- Subordinate: "That's an interesting approach. Have you considered other options?"

- Dominant: "Oh, I'm sure you'll make the right decision. You always do."

The dominant character's words appear supportive but may carry a patronizing or pressuring undertone.

5. Leverage Silence

What isn't said can be just as impactful as what is. Silence, interrupted sentences, or changes in subject can suggest discomfort, defiance, or suppressed emotions.

Example:

- Dialogue: "Why didn't you call me back?"

- Response: "I was busy." (Followed by a long pause).

The silence following the response suggests avoidance or guilt, adding depth to the interaction.

6. Foreshadow Through Subtext

Use subtext to hint at future events or conflicts. This technique adds layers of meaning that become clear as the story unfolds.

Example:

- Dialogue: "Don't forget the last time we trusted someone like him."

The subtext foreshadows potential betrayal or conflict, creating tension and intrigue.

7. Play with Expectations

Contradicting expectations in dialogue can create humor, tension, or surprise, revealing subtext in unexpected ways.

Example:

- Character A: "I thought you'd be happy for me."
- Character B: "Oh, I am. Thrilled." (Said flatly, while staring at their drink).

The contrast between Character B's words and tone suggests jealousy or bitterness.

Exercises to Practice Subtext

1. **Rewrite Explicit Dialogue:** Take a piece of dialogue that explicitly states emotions or intentions and rewrite it with subtext. Focus on tone, body language, and implied meaning.

    o Original: "I'm nervous about this interview."

  o Subtext: "Do you think this tie makes me look confident?" (Paired with fidgeting).

2. **Create a Scene with Hidden Tensions:** Write a conversation between two characters who are angry with each other but trying to appear polite. Use subtext to show their emotions without having them directly address the conflict.

3. **Practice with Silence:** Write a dialogue where one character's silence or minimal responses carry significant meaning. Experiment with pacing and pauses to create tension.

4. **Use Props to Convey Subtext:** Write a scene where a character interacts with an object while speaking, using their actions to reveal underlying emotions. For example, a character might repeatedly adjust their watch while discussing a sensitive topic, hinting at impatience or anxiety.

5. **Analyze Real Conversations:** Observe or listen to real-life conversations, noting instances where people use subtext. Practice incorporating similar nuances into your writing.

Conclusion

Subtext in dialogue is a powerful tool for conveying emotions and intentions in a nuanced and engaging way. By using body language, tone, pauses, and context, writers can create layered conversations that feel authentic and dynamic. Practicing these techniques will help you master the art of subtext, adding depth and richness to your storytelling.

Body Language and Reactions

Body language and reactions are powerful tools for conveying a character's internal state without relying on direct exposition. Non-verbal cues like posture, facial expressions, gestures, and physical responses can reveal emotions, intentions, and personality traits in a way that feels natural and engaging. Mastering this aspect of storytelling allows writers to "show" rather than "tell," drawing readers deeper into the narrative.

Using Non-Verbal Cues to Show Internal States

Characters' physical actions often speak louder than words, offering subtle yet impactful insights into their thoughts and feelings. By observing how a character moves, reacts, or interacts with their environment, readers can infer their emotional state and motivations.

1. Facial Expressions

The face is a rich source of emotional expression. Characters' eyes, mouth, and overall expressions can reveal a range of emotions, from joy to fear to anger.

Example:

- **Explicit:** She was angry.

- **With Non-Verbal Cues:** Her lips pressed into a thin line, and her brows drew together as her glare bore into him.

The second example avoids directly stating the emotion, instead using physical description to show it.

2. Posture and Stance

A character's posture can convey confidence, insecurity, or fatigue. Slouched shoulders might indicate defeat or exhaustion, while an upright stance suggests confidence or attentiveness.

Example:

- **Confident:** He entered the room with his chin held high, shoulders squared, and each step measured and deliberate.

- **Insecure:** She lingered near the doorway, her arms crossed tightly over her chest, eyes darting around the room.

Posture creates a vivid image that allows readers to understand the character's mindset without needing further explanation.

3. Gestures

Small, repeated gestures can provide clues about a character's emotional state. Nervous habits, such as fidgeting or tapping, often reveal unease, while deliberate hand movements might indicate decisiveness or control.

Example:

- **Nervous:** His fingers drummed an erratic rhythm against the tabletop, the sound quickening as the silence stretched.

- **Calm:** She placed her hand gently over the child's, her touch steady and reassuring.

Gestures not only enhance characterization but also create dynamic and visually engaging scenes.

4. Interactions with Objects

The way characters handle objects can reflect their emotions. A nervous character might fiddle with a pen, while an angry character might slam a door or crush a paper cup.

Example:

- **Frustration:** She shoved the stack of papers off the desk, the sheets scattering across the floor like fallen leaves.

- **Anticipation:** He ran his thumb over the edge of the ticket, the movement slow and deliberate, as if savoring the moment.

These interactions add texture to scenes, subtly reinforcing the character's state of mind.

5. Physiological Reactions

Physical responses, such as a racing heartbeat or sweaty palms, can convey intense emotions like fear or excitement. These reactions are especially effective in high-stakes or emotionally charged moments.

Example:

- **Fear:** Her pulse thundered in her ears, and her breath came in shallow, rapid bursts as she pressed herself against the wall.

- **Excitement:** His chest swelled with each breath, and his hands trembled as he reached for the envelope.

Physiological cues immerse readers in the character's experience, making emotions feel immediate and visceral.

Examples and Analysis

Let's analyze specific examples of body language and reactions in different emotional contexts to understand how they enhance storytelling.

1. Fear and Anxiety

Example:

- She gripped the edge of the table so tightly her knuckles turned white. Her eyes darted to the window, and a bead of sweat traced a path down her temple.

Analysis: This description uses physical tension (gripping the table), a physiological response (sweating), and eye movement (darting) to convey the character's fear. The reader can sense her anxiety without needing it spelled out.

2. Joy and Excitement

Example:

- He threw his arms into the air, a wide grin splitting his face as he let out a jubilant whoop that echoed through the hall.

Analysis: The energetic gestures (throwing arms up) and auditory response (whoop) vividly illustrate the character's joy. The reader can feel the excitement through the dynamic description.

3. Sadness and Grief

Example:

- Her shoulders sagged, and she stared at the photograph in her hands. A single tear slipped down her cheek, unnoticed as her thumb traced the frame's edge.

Analysis: The drooping posture (sagging shoulders) and delicate action (tracing the frame) create a poignant image of grief. The tear, described subtly, enhances the emotional impact without overtly stating her sadness.

4. Anger and Frustration

Example:

- His jaw clenched, and his fists tightened at his sides. When he spoke, his voice was low and taut, each word a struggle against the storm brewing inside.

Analysis: The clenched jaw and fists physically demonstrate anger, while the controlled tone of voice suggests the character is trying to contain his frustration. This layered description makes the emotion feel raw and authentic.

5. Love and Affection

Example:

- She brushed a stray lock of hair from his forehead, her fingers lingering for a moment longer than necessary. Her smile was soft, her gaze steady and warm.

Analysis: The gentle touch and lingering gesture convey affection, while the smile and steady gaze reinforce the emotion. The reader can sense the character's tenderness through these understated cues.

Crafting Effective Body Language and Reactions

To use body language and reactions effectively, consider the following tips:

1. Be Specific

Vague descriptions like "he looked nervous" or "she was happy" lack impact. Instead, focus on specific actions or reactions that convey the emotion.

Example:

- **Vague:** She seemed nervous.

- **Specific:** She twisted the hem of her shirt, her eyes darting toward the clock every few seconds.

2. Match the Emotion's Intensity

Ensure that the body language matches the degree of emotion the character is experiencing. Subtle cues work well for mild emotions, while stronger reactions are appropriate for intense moments.

Example:

- **Subtle:** He tapped his foot lightly, his gaze flicking to the door.

- **Intense:** He paced the room, his hands tugging at his hair as his breaths came fast and shallow.

3. Avoid Overloading the Scene

While body language adds depth, too many cues can overwhelm the reader. Focus on a few key actions or reactions to keep the description concise and impactful.

Example:

- **Overloaded:** She crossed her arms, tapped her foot, sighed heavily, and rolled her eyes, all while glaring at him.

- **Effective:** She crossed her arms and tapped her foot, her glare sharp enough to cut.

4. Consider Context

Body language should be appropriate to the scene and the character's personality. A reserved character might show anger through a clenched jaw, while an expressive one might shout or gesture wildly.

5. Use Contrast for Complexity

Contradictory cues can reveal inner conflict or hidden emotions. For example, a character might smile while clenching their fists, suggesting they are masking anger with politeness.

Example:

- Her lips curved into a smile, but her hands tightened into fists beneath the table.

Exercises for Practicing Body Language and Reactions

1. **Emotion Focus:** Write a scene where a character experiences a strong emotion (e.g., fear, joy, anger) using only body language and reactions to convey it.

2. **Silent Argument:** Create a dialogue-free scene where two characters argue through gestures, posture, and facial expressions.

3. **Layered Reactions:** Write a scene where a character feels one emotion outwardly but another internally. Use contrasting body language to show the conflict.

4. **Object Interaction:** Have a character's interaction with an object reveal their mood. For instance, how they handle a cup of coffee can indicate impatience, calm, or nervousness.

Conclusion

Body language and reactions are essential tools for showing internal states in a dynamic and authentic way. By focusing on non-verbal cues such as facial expressions, posture, gestures, and physiological responses, writers can create nuanced and emotionally resonant scenes. Practicing these techniques will help you develop characters that feel alive and relatable, drawing readers deeper into your story.

Chapter Four

Crafting Vivid Settings

World-Building Through Showing

World-building is the foundation of immersive storytelling, enabling readers to step into a vivid and believable world. While exposition and direct description have their place, the most engaging worlds are those revealed naturally through the narrative. Integrating the setting organically and showing the mood and tone of a place creates a seamless and immersive experience for readers, allowing them to explore and interpret the world alongside the characters.

Integrating Setting Naturally Into the Narrative

To build a world through showing, writers must weave the setting into the actions, dialogue, and experiences of the characters. This approach avoids overwhelming the reader with lengthy descriptions while maintaining the story's momentum.

1. Use Character Interactions with the Setting

One of the most effective ways to reveal a setting is through a character's interaction with it. How characters engage with their surroundings can convey details about the environment and their place within it.

Example:

- Instead of: "The marketplace was a bustling hub of activity with colorful stalls and loud vendors."

- Try: "Lila ducked under a string of lanterns, the aroma of spiced meat drawing her toward a stall where a vendor shouted, 'Fresh skewers! Five for a coin!' She sidestepped a boy balancing a crate of oranges and caught her reflection in a silver trinket hanging from a nearby cart."

In this example, the marketplace comes to life through Lila's actions and sensory experiences, giving the reader a vivid picture without halting the narrative.

2. Reveal Through Dialogue

Characters' conversations can hint at the setting without needing explicit description. This approach also allows for the inclusion of cultural and societal details.

Example:

- Dialogue: "If we don't reach the gates before sundown, the patrols will lock us out. You know what happened to Maren last week."

This brief exchange conveys that the city is heavily guarded, possibly dangerous, and enforces strict rules about entry times, all without directly stating these facts.

3. Embed Details in Action

Setting details can be revealed through characters' actions, making the environment an active part of the narrative rather than static background.

Example:

- Instead of: "The library was enormous, with towering shelves packed with ancient books."

- Try: "Elena craned her neck to read the faded titles on the highest shelf, her fingers brushing against the thick layer of dust that clung to the spines."

The action of brushing dust off the books implies the library's age and disuse while grounding the description in the character's experience.

4. Focus on Specific, Meaningful Details

Rather than cataloging every aspect of a setting, select a few details that resonate emotionally or symbolically with the scene or characters.

Example:

- "The cabin's single window framed a view of the forest, where bare branches clawed at the grey sky. Inside, the air carried the faint tang of woodsmoke and mildew."

These details establish the mood and tone while leaving room for the reader's imagination to fill in the rest.

5. Let the Setting Shape the Plot

The world should feel like a living entity that influences the characters and story. Natural obstacles, cultural norms, or environmental challenges can drive conflict and reveal the setting organically.

Example:

- "The river had swelled overnight, its muddy waters swallowing the narrow bridge they'd planned to cross. 'We'll have to take the long way,' Sam said, tightening his pack straps. 'If the wolves don't get us first.'"

Here, the environment creates a problem for the characters while providing insight into the setting's dangers.

Showing the Mood and Tone of a Place

The mood and tone of a setting influence how readers perceive the world and the story's emotional atmosphere. Using sensory details, symbolic imagery, and the characters' reactions can help establish these elements.

1. Use Sensory Details

Engage the reader's senses to create an immersive experience. Each sense contributes to the mood, whether it's the oppressive heat of a desert or the muffled silence of a snow-covered forest.

Example:

- "The air inside the cave was damp and heavy, carrying the metallic tang of wet stone. Droplets fell in rhythmic drips, echoing through the darkness as if the cave itself were alive."

The sensory details evoke a claustrophobic and eerie mood, matching the tone of a mysterious or dangerous environment.

2. Choose Symbolic Imagery

Imagery can reflect the emotional undertones of a scene, reinforcing its mood and tone.

Example:

- "In the heart of the abandoned village, shutters hung crookedly from their hinges, swaying in the wind like mourners at a funeral. The ground was littered with broken pottery, fragments of lives long forgotten."

The imagery of decay and loss emphasizes a somber, haunting tone, enhancing the emotional impact of the scene.

3. Align Setting with Characters' Emotions

Let the environment mirror or contrast with a character's emotional state to deepen the reader's understanding of their inner world.

Example:

- Mirror: "The rain lashed against the windows, matching the turmoil churning in her chest."

- Contrast: "The sun blazed overhead, indifferent to the cold knot of dread tightening in his stomach."

This technique ties the setting to the character's perspective, making the scene more intimate and impactful.

4. Vary the Atmosphere

Use changes in the setting to reflect shifts in mood or tone, keeping the world dynamic and responsive to the story.

Example:

- At the beginning of a journey: "The morning sun bathed the valley in gold, and the breeze carried the sweet scent of wildflowers."

- After a devastating loss: "The valley lay under a blanket of mist, its colors muted and lifeless in the grey dawn."

By altering the atmosphere, the setting becomes an active participant in the story's emotional arc.

5. Incorporate Cultural and Historical Context

Details about a setting's culture, history, or societal norms can add richness and depth while influencing the mood.

Example:

- "The plaza was lined with statues of past rulers, their faces worn smooth by centuries of wind and rain. Vendors hawked their wares beneath faded banners, their voices tinged with urgency as storm clouds gathered on the horizon."

This description hints at the setting's history and impending danger, adding layers of meaning to the scene.

Examples and Analysis

1. Fantasy Setting

Example:

- "The forest glowed faintly in the moonlight, its leaves shimmering like silver scales. A distant howl pierced the stillness, sending a flock of birds spiraling into the sky. Beneath the canopy, the air was thick with the scent of damp earth and blooming nightshade."

Analysis: This description uses sensory details (sight, sound, smell) to establish an otherworldly and slightly ominous tone. The shimmering leaves and eerie howl suggest a magical yet dangerous environment.

2. Urban Setting

Example:

- "Neon signs buzzed against the darkened sky, their garish colors reflected in puddles that lined the cracked sidewalks. The air smelled of gasoline and fried food, and the chatter of passing strangers blended with the distant wail of a siren."

Analysis: The sensory details paint a vivid picture of a gritty urban environment. The mood is chaotic and unpolished, emphasizing the vibrancy and harshness of city life.

3. Historical Setting

Example:

- "The castle's stone walls loomed high above the village, their surfaces etched with the scars of ancient battles. Torches flickered in iron sconces, casting long shadows that danced across the cobblestone streets. The clatter of hooves echoed in the narrow alleys, accompanied by the faint strains of a lute from the tavern."

Analysis: This description combines visual imagery (stone walls, shadows) with sounds (hooves, lute) to evoke a medieval atmosphere. The historical context enriches the setting, making it feel authentic and lived-in.

Exercises for Practice

1. **Action-Based Description:** Write a scene where a character navigates a busy marketplace. Focus on revealing the setting through their interactions with vendors, objects, and other shoppers.

2. **Mood Matching:** Describe a setting that reflects a character's grief. Use sensory details and symbolic imagery to convey the emotional tone.

3. **Dynamic Setting:** Write two descriptions of the same place—one during a joyful festival and another after a tragedy. Highlight how changes in the environment alter the mood and tone.

4. **Cultural Depth:** Create a setting that reflects a unique culture or history. Show these elements through architecture, traditions, or dialogue without explicitly explaining them.

Conclusion

World-building through showing integrates the setting into the narrative organically, allowing readers to discover the world naturally alongside the characters. By using sensory details, symbolic imagery, and dynamic environments, writers can establish mood and tone while keeping the story immersive and engaging. Practicing these techniques will help you create rich, compelling worlds that captivate your audience and bring your story to life.

Using the Environment to Reflect Characters

The environment in a story can serve as a powerful mirror to characters' emotions, internal conflicts, and personal growth. When the setting resonates with a character's state of mind or journey, it enhances the narrative by deepening the emotional impact and tying the external world to the internal one. By thoughtfully linking the environment to characters, writers can create scenes that are both visually evocative and emotionally resonant.

Linking Setting to Character Emotions

The environment can echo a character's feelings, making their emotional state more tangible to readers. Whether through natural landscapes, urban backdrops, or intimate interiors, the setting becomes an extension of the character's inner world.

1. Reflecting Joy and Optimism

A bright, lively setting can amplify a character's feelings of happiness or hope. Use vivid imagery and positive sensory details to create a sense of alignment between the character's emotions and their surroundings.

Example:

- As Clara skipped through the orchard, sunlight dappled the ground, and the air hummed with the chatter of sparrows. The blossoms above her swayed gently, their pink petals drifting like tiny dancers in the breeze.

Analysis: The warm and vibrant imagery mirrors Clara's joyful mood, reinforcing the harmony between her inner feelings and the external world.

2. Mirroring Sadness or Grief

A somber or desolate setting can emphasize a character's sadness or sense of loss. The environment's emptiness or decay can serve as a metaphor for the character's emotional void.

Example:

- The once-bustling pier was silent now, its wooden planks warped and splintered from years of neglect. Waves lapped listlessly against the posts, and a grey mist hung low, blurring the horizon. Anna stood at the edge, clutching her coat tighter against the chill.

Analysis: The desolate pier reflects Anna's feelings of isolation and sorrow, with the neglected surroundings acting as a visual representation of her inner desolation.

3. Projecting Anger or Turmoil

Chaotic or intense environments can mirror a character's anger or inner turmoil. Storms, wildfires, or crowded, noisy streets can serve as external manifestations of emotional conflict.

Example:

- The storm raged around him, wind howling through the treetops and rain lashing against his skin. Thunder cracked overhead as he yelled into the void, his voice swallowed by the tempest.

Analysis: The storm's fury mirrors the character's internal anger, creating a visceral connection between the character's emotions and their surroundings.

4. Enhancing Fear or Anxiety

An oppressive or foreboding setting can heighten a character's fear or unease. Darkness, confined spaces, or eerie silence can amplify the tension.

Example:

- The hallway stretched endlessly before her, the flickering fluorescent lights casting jagged shadows on the peeling wallpaper. Each step echoed unnaturally, as if the building itself were holding its breath.

Analysis: The unsettling environment reflects the character's fear, immersing the reader in their anxiety and anticipation.

Using Setting to Highlight Character Growth

As characters evolve over the course of a story, their interactions with the environment can reflect their personal development. Changes in setting can symbolize transformation, resolve, or newfound understanding.

1. From Chaos to Order

A disorganized or hostile environment that gradually becomes more harmonious can symbolize a character's journey from turmoil to clarity or peace.

Example:

- At the start of the story: "The apartment was a cluttered mess, with stacks of unopened mail spilling onto the floor and dishes piling precariously in the sink."

- By the end: "The apartment was clean and inviting, sunlight streaming through freshly washed windows. A vase of wildflowers brightened the coffee table, their fragrance filling the air."

Analysis: The transformation of the space mirrors the character's internal growth, showing how they've regained control over their life.

2. Nature as a Symbol of Rebirth

Natural settings can symbolize renewal or self-discovery, particularly when characters engage with these environments during moments of change.

Example:

- "She stepped into the clearing, where the first rays of dawn lit the dewdrops on the grass like tiny jewels. The air was crisp and filled with the scent of pine, and for the first time in months, she felt as if she could breathe."

Analysis: The serene and rejuvenating environment reflects the character's newfound sense of hope and healing.

3. Overcoming Fear Through Setting

When a character confronts a challenging environment and emerges victorious, it can symbolize personal courage and growth.

Example:

- "The cave was as dark and suffocating as she'd imagined, its narrow passages pressing in from all sides. But with each step forward, her breathing steadied, and the weight of her fear began to lift. By the time she reached the chamber at its heart, she felt lighter, as if she'd left her doubts behind in the shadows."

Analysis: The character's journey through the intimidating environment symbolizes her inner strength and ability to overcome her fears.

4. The Past and the Present

Returning to a familiar setting can highlight how much a character has changed. Contrasting their current perspective with their past experiences in the same place underscores personal growth.

Example:

- "The schoolyard looked smaller than she remembered. The swings still creaked in the breeze, and the old oak tree still stood tall, its branches reaching skyward. But where she once felt invisible among the cliques of children, she now walked confidently across the grass, her steps sure and steady."

Analysis: The unchanged environment serves as a backdrop to emphasize the character's transformation, illustrating how far they've come.

Techniques for Linking Setting and Character

1. Use Symbolism

Choose elements of the environment that resonate symbolically with the character's journey. A broken mirror might reflect fragmented self-perception, while a blooming garden could symbolize growth and renewal.

2. Write from the Character's Perspective

Describe the setting through the character's eyes, letting their emotions shape the way they perceive the environment.

Example:

- A character feeling lonely might describe a bustling city street as cold and impersonal, while another feeling inspired might see it as vibrant and full of possibilities.

3. Show Contrast Over Time

Revisit the same setting at different points in the story to highlight changes in the character's perspective or emotions.

Example:

- Early in the story: "The forest was dark and oppressive, the twisted roots seeming to claw at her boots with every step."

- Later: "The forest was alive with birdsong, sunlight filtering through the leaves in golden shafts. She ran her fingers over the bark of a tree, feeling its strength and warmth."

4. Match or Oppose the Mood

Decide whether the setting should align with the character's emotions (e.g., a storm during a heated argument) or contrast with them (e.g., a sunny day during a moment of despair). Both approaches can be effective, depending on the story's needs.

Exercises for Practice

1. **Emotional Reflection:** Write a scene where a character's environment mirrors their emotions. Use sensory details to enhance the connection.

2. **Symbolic Transformation:** Describe a setting that changes alongside a character's growth. Focus on how the changes reflect their journey.

3. **Contrasting Perspectives:** Write two descriptions of the same setting, one from the perspective of a character at their lowest point and another from the perspective of the same character after achieving a personal breakthrough.

4. **Conflict in the Environment:** Create a scene where the setting adds tension to a character's internal conflict. For example, a storm might heighten feelings of fear or urgency.

Conclusion

By linking the environment to characters' emotions and growth, writers can create rich, multilayered narratives that resonate with readers on a deeper level. Thoughtfully crafted settings not only enhance the story's atmosphere but also serve as a lens through which readers can understand the characters' inner worlds. Practicing these techniques will help you master the art of using the environment as an active and meaningful element in your storytelling.

Exercises: Writing Dynamic Descriptions

Dynamic descriptions that blend action and setting details can transform a static narrative into an engaging, immersive experience. These descriptions provide not only a vivid sense of place but also a sense of movement and purpose, tying characters to their surroundings in meaningful ways. The following exercises are designed to help you practice crafting dynamic descriptions that integrate setting and action seamlessly.

The Importance of Blending Action and Setting

Incorporating action into your descriptions of the environment ensures that your scenes feel alive and immediate. Rather than pausing the narrative for blocks of static description, blending the two keeps the story moving while still painting a vivid picture for the reader.

Example of Static Description:

"The forest was dense, filled with towering trees and thick underbrush. The air was damp and smelled of moss and earth."

Example of Dynamic Description:

"Branches snagged at her sleeves as she pushed through the dense underbrush. The damp air clung to her skin, heavy with the scent of moss and earth, while the rustle of unseen creatures echoed around her."

The second example combines action with sensory details, immersing the reader in the character's experience while still describing the setting.

Exercise 1: Action-Oriented Setting Description

Write a scene where a character interacts with their environment in a way that reveals key details about the setting. Focus on using the character's actions to bring the scene to life.

Prompt:

- A traveler arrives at a bustling marketplace.

Example: "She dodged a cart laden with brightly colored fabrics, its wheels creaking under the weight. The air buzzed with the voices of merchants calling out their wares, mingling with the sharp clink of coins exchanging hands. She sidestepped a boy carrying a basket of fruit, nearly stumbling over a stray dog weaving through the crowd."

Tips:

- Use specific, sensory-rich details.

- Avoid pausing the narrative to describe; instead, let the description emerge through the character's movements.

Exercise 2: Setting as an Obstacle

Create a scene where the setting itself presents a challenge or obstacle for the character. Use action to show how the environment impacts their progress or decisions.

Prompt:

- A storm hits while a character is hiking in the mountains.

Example: "The wind howled through the narrow pass, whipping her hair into her eyes. She squinted against the driving rain, each step a battle against the slippery rocks beneath her boots. Lightning split the sky, illuminating jagged cliffs that seemed to close in around her."

Tips:

- Highlight the interaction between the character and the setting.

- Show how the environment shapes the character's actions and emotions.

Exercise 3: Revealing Emotion Through Setting

Write a description that reflects a character's emotional state through their interaction with the environment. Let the setting mirror or contrast with their mood.

Prompt:

- A character revisits a childhood home.

Example: "She hesitated on the creaking porch, her fingers trailing along the chipped paint of the railing. The once-bright yellow shutters were now faded and askew, and weeds pushed through the cracks in the front steps. She stepped inside, the familiar scent of cedar and dust wrapping around her like an old memory she wasn't sure she wanted to relive."

Tips:

- Use symbolic or evocative details to reflect the character's feelings.

- Avoid directly stating emotions; instead, let them emerge through the description.

Exercise 4: Dynamic Dialogue and Description

Combine dialogue with action and setting description to create a scene that feels alive and multifaceted.

Prompt:

- Two characters argue while preparing a meal in a small kitchen.

Example: "'You never listen to me,' she snapped, slamming the pot onto the stove. The scent of garlic and onions sizzling in the pan filled the cramped kitchen, mixing with the sharp tang of her frustration. He leaned against the counter, arms crossed, the edge of the cutting board digging into his side. 'Maybe if you made sense once in a while,' he retorted, the knife in his hand slicing through a carrot with sharp, precise strokes."

Tips:

- Use the setting to enhance the tension or mood.

- Show characters' emotions through their actions and interactions with the environment.

Exercise 5: Shifting Perspectives

Write a description of the same setting from two different characters' perspectives. Focus on how their actions and interpretations of the environment reveal their personalities and priorities.

Prompt:

- Two travelers explore an abandoned castle.

Example (Character A): "He ran his fingers over the crumbling stone wall, marveling at the intricate carvings half-hidden by ivy. His footsteps echoed in the vast, empty hall, and he paused to gaze up at the stained glass window, its colors muted but still breathtaking."

Example (Character B): "She tightened her grip on the flashlight, its narrow beam cutting through the shadows. Every creak of the floorboards made her flinch, and she kept glancing over her shoulder, certain they weren't alone in the silent, drafty corridors."

Tips:

- Let each character's perception of the setting reflect their personality and emotional state.

- Use contrasting details to highlight their differences.

Exercise 6: Time and Transformation

Describe how a setting changes over time, using action to show the passage of time and its effects on the environment.

Prompt:

- A park transitions from morning to evening.

Example: "In the morning, the park buzzed with activity— joggers pounding along the paths, children's laughter ringing out from the playground, and dogs chasing sticks through the dew-dappled grass. By evening, the park had grown quiet, the once-bright sky now streaked with deep oranges and purples. The streetlamps flickered on one by one, their light pooling in soft circles on the empty paths."

Tips:

- Use the setting's transformation to create a sense of movement and continuity.

- Incorporate sensory details to evoke different times of day.

Exercise 7: Setting as a Character

Write a scene where the setting feels like an active participant in the story, shaping events and influencing characters as though it has its own personality.

Prompt:

- A haunted house resists the intruders exploring it.

Example: "The door groaned in protest as they pushed it open, a cold draft sweeping through the hall to snuff out their candles. The wallpaper peeled in long, curling strips, as if recoiling from their presence. Every step on the staircase elicited a sharp creak, and the shadows seemed to deepen, watching, waiting."

Tips:

- Use personification to give the setting agency.

- Let the environment actively influence the characters' actions and emotions.

Conclusion

Dynamic descriptions that blend action and setting details add depth and immediacy to your writing. By practicing these exercises, you can develop the skills to create immersive, engaging scenes where the environment and characters are interconnected. Remember to focus on movement, sensory details, and the relationship between the setting and the narrative to bring your stories to life.

Chapter Five

Evoking Emotion

Showing Emotional States

Emotion is at the heart of compelling storytelling. The ability to evoke emotions authentically is what connects readers to characters and their journeys. Showing emotional states effectively means moving beyond clichés and generic descriptions to craft moments that resonate deeply. This involves employing physical reactions, internal thoughts, and dialogue to convey a character's inner world.

Avoiding Clichés in Emotional Descriptions

Clichés in emotional descriptions are overused phrases that fail to evoke genuine feelings. For instance, "her heart raced" or "he felt a lump in his throat" are commonly seen in narratives but often lack originality and depth.

1. **Recognizing Clichés**

   o Phrases like "butterflies in the stomach" or "knees turned to jelly" may come to mind quickly because they're familiar, but they often feel generic.

   o Clichés signal to the reader what to feel rather than immersing them in the experience.

2. **Reimagining Emotional Reactions**

o Instead of relying on the expected, think of unique ways to describe emotional states. For instance, instead of "her heart raced," you could write, "The pulse in her neck pounded so hard she was sure it would echo in the room."

o Use sensory details that are specific to the character or situation.

3. **Grounding Emotion in Context**

o Consider the circumstances of the scene. How would a particular character uniquely experience fear, anger, or joy? Their profession, age, background, and personality can influence how they perceive and react emotionally.

Example:

- **Cliché:** "He was shaking with fear."

- **Reimagined:** "His hands trembled as he fumbled with the doorknob, the slickness of sweat making it impossible to grip."

Using Physical Reactions to Convey Feelings

Physical reactions are a powerful way to show emotions without explicitly stating them. The body often betrays what the mind tries to hide, and these subtle clues can bring scenes to life.

1. **Non-Verbal Cues**

o   Tense muscles, clenched fists, quickened breath, or averted eyes can reveal emotions like anger, nervousness, or guilt.

o   Micro-expressions, like a flicker of surprise or a fleeting frown, can hint at deeper feelings.

2. **Matching Reactions to Intensity**

o   Small emotions may manifest in subtle ways: a slight twitch of the lips, a deep exhale. Larger emotions might provoke exaggerated movements, like pacing or yelling.

o   Align the physical reaction with the intensity of the emotion to maintain believability.

3. **Contradictory Signals**

o   Adding complexity by showing conflicting emotions can make characters more realistic. For example, a character might laugh nervously while their hands grip the edge of a table.

Example:

- A character learning devastating news might not immediately burst into tears. Instead, they could sit frozen, their fingers curling into the fabric of their coat as their breath slows unnaturally.

Using Thoughts to Reveal Internal Conflict

While physical reactions show surface emotions, internal thoughts can reveal the deeper, often contradictory feelings a character might have. This combination adds richness to emotional states.

1. **Stream of Consciousness**

   o Dive into the character's immediate thoughts. Are they trying to rationalize their fear? Are they conflicted about how they feel? Use these moments to show their internal battle.

2. **Layered Feelings**

   o People rarely experience one emotion at a time. A character might feel anger laced with sadness or excitement tinged with dread. Internal thoughts can capture these nuances.

3. **Avoid Over-Exposition**

   o Keep internal thoughts focused and impactful. Long, rambling internal monologues can dilute the emotion instead of amplifying it.

Example:

- Instead of "She felt betrayed," write: "How could he do this? After everything they'd been through, every promise he'd made, he'd turned his back on her."

Using Dialogue to Show Emotion

Dialogue is a natural way to reveal emotions, often in a character's choice of words, tone, or even what they leave unsaid.

1. **Subtext in Speech**

   o   What characters say can often differ from what they feel. For instance, a character who is heartbroken might insist, "I'm fine," while their tone and body language suggest otherwise.

2. **Tone and Cadence**

   o   The rhythm and tone of dialogue can convey emotions. Short, clipped sentences might indicate anger or urgency, while long, rambling sentences could suggest nervousness or excitement.

3. **Dialogue Tags and Beats**

   o   Avoid relying heavily on tags like "she said angrily" or "he replied happily." Instead, use actions or body language to complement the dialogue.

   o   For example, instead of:

      ▪   "I'm not scared," he said defensively.

   o   Write:

      ▪   "I'm not scared." He crossed his arms and leaned back, avoiding her gaze.

Example:

- **Subtext in Dialogue:**

   o   "So...you're leaving again?"

- o "Just for a while. You know how it is."

- o "Sure, I know how it is." She smiled, but her fingers dug into the counter.

Combining Techniques for Emotional Depth

To fully immerse the reader in a character's emotional state, combine physical reactions, internal thoughts, and dialogue. This layered approach makes emotions feel authentic and multifaceted.

Example Scene:

- **Telling:** "He was furious."

- **Showing:**

    - o He slammed the mug onto the table, the coffee sloshing over the rim. His jaw tightened as he stared at the stain spreading across the wood. *How many times had she promised not to interfere?* "You couldn't help yourself, could you?" His voice was low, controlled, but his knuckles whitened as his fist clenched.

Practical Tips and Exercises

1. **Emotion Mapping**

    - o Choose a key emotion and list physical reactions, internal thoughts, and dialogue that could convey it. Avoid clichés and think of creative alternatives.

2. **Rewrite Telling Sentences**

   o   Take sentences like "She was nervous" and rewrite them using physical reactions and thoughts. For example:

      ▪   Original: "She was nervous about the interview."

      ▪   Revised: "Her palms felt clammy as she smoothed the hem of her skirt for the third time. She rehearsed her opening line in her head, but the words jumbled together in a way that made her stomach churn."

3. **Layered Emotion Practice**

   o   Write a scene where a character feels two conflicting emotions, such as relief and guilt, or love and fear. Focus on showing both emotions through their actions and inner world.

4. **Dialogue Subtext Drill**

   o   Write a conversation where the characters don't explicitly state how they feel, but their words and tone suggest their emotions. For example:

      ▪   "You didn't wait for me."

      ▪   "I thought you wouldn't mind."

      ▪   "I see. Well, next time, maybe ask."

Why Showing Emotional States Matters

Showing emotions instead of telling them deepens the reader's connection to the story. It allows readers to experience the moment alongside the characters, rather than being told what to feel. This active engagement creates a more immersive and satisfying reading experience.

By focusing on physical reactions, thoughts, and dialogue, you can craft emotional scenes that feel genuine and leave a lasting impact. Remember, the goal is not to over-explain, but to trust the reader to interpret the clues you provide. When done well, showing emotional states becomes one of the most powerful tools in a writer's arsenal.

Building Tension and Suspense

Tension and suspense are the lifeblood of compelling storytelling, keeping readers on the edge of their seats and urging them to turn the page. Mastering these elements requires subtlety, precision, and the ability to show stakes and escalate conflict without explicitly spelling everything out. In this section, we'll explore how to build tension effectively, show the stakes, and use techniques that escalate conflict to grip readers until the very end.

Showing the Stakes Without Overtly Stating Them

The stakes in your story—the risks or potential consequences faced by your characters—create the foundation for tension. Rather than explicitly stating what's at risk, showing the stakes through action, behavior, and subtext allows readers to experience the tension more vividly.

1. **Use the Environment to Reflect Stakes**

    o   The setting can hint at impending danger or high stakes without overtly declaring them. For example, a character in a crumbling house during a storm conveys peril without needing narration like, "She was in danger of the house collapsing."

    o   Small details, like the groaning of wooden beams or a flickering lightbulb, subtly reinforce the stakes.

2. **Show Emotional Reactions**

- o Characters' physical and emotional responses can reveal the gravity of a situation. If a protagonist's voice trembles, their palms sweat, or their gaze darts around a room, it suggests tension without needing direct explanation.

3. **Dramatic Irony**

   - o Letting the audience know more than the characters builds a natural tension. For example, if a character unknowingly walks toward a room where danger lurks, the stakes become clear to the reader through context, not exposition.

4. **Symbolism and Foreshadowing**

   - o Use objects, gestures, or dialogue to hint at what's at stake. A wedding ring carelessly placed on a table can symbolize a faltering relationship without stating, "Their marriage was in trouble."

Example:

- Instead of writing, "The test was important to her future," show the stakes:

  - o She traced her finger along the dog-eared pages of her textbook, her heart racing as the clock ticked louder with every second.

Techniques for Escalating Conflict

Conflict drives a story forward, and tension peaks when the stakes continually rise. Escalating conflict requires careful pacing, layering of challenges, and making the audience feel like the situation is spiraling out of control.

1. **Introduce Complications**

    o Every time a character overcomes a hurdle, introduce another. These complications can range from external obstacles (a locked door, a rival) to internal dilemmas (self-doubt, conflicting emotions).

    o For instance, if a character is rushing to deliver an important package, an unforeseen roadblock—like a flat tire or a lost address—escalates the situation.

2. **Pace Your Reveals**

    o Instead of laying out all the information at once, drip-feed details to the reader. This creates an air of mystery and anticipation.

    o For example, a character might overhear a fragment of a conversation that hints at betrayal. The full truth doesn't come out until later, keeping the tension simmering.

3. **Heighten Emotional Stakes**

    o External challenges become more impactful when paired with emotional stakes. If a character must defuse a bomb, the situation becomes even more tense if they're on the phone with their family at the same time, knowing this might be their last conversation.

4. **Use Short Sentences and Pacing**

   o During moments of high tension, shorter sentences and fragmented thoughts can mimic the frantic pace of a character's mind. This creates urgency and mirrors the rising stakes.

   o Example:

     ▪ The door creaked.

     ▪ She froze.

     ▪ Another sound—closer this time.

5. **Let the Reader's Imagination Work**

   o Often, what's left unsaid is more terrifying than what's stated. By allowing readers to fill in gaps, you engage their imagination and amplify suspense. For example, describing the shadows in a forest as "alive with shifting shapes" invites readers to conjure their own fears.

Building Tension in Different Types of Stories

1. **Mystery and Thriller**

   o These genres thrive on unanswered questions. Introduce clues that lead the protagonist (and the reader) toward the truth, but keep them guessing until the climax.

o   Example:

- A detective finds a bloodstained scarf at a crime scene. It doesn't belong to the victim—but who does it belong to, and why is it there?

2. **Romance**

o   Tension in romance often stems from will-they-won't-they dynamics or misunderstandings. Build tension through lingering glances, half-spoken words, or external forces that keep the lovers apart.

o   Example:

- Two characters stand inches apart, neither daring to cross the invisible line between friendship and something more. The air between them crackles with unspoken possibilities.

3. **Horror**

o   Fear of the unknown is a powerful tool. Reveal only fragments of the threat—a creak in the floorboards, a flicker of movement in the shadows—to build suspense.

o   Example:

- The basement light flickered and died. For a moment, the silence was absolute. Then came the scrape of metal against concrete.

4. **Fantasy and Science Fiction**

- o Tension in speculative genres often involves high-stakes battles, magical or technological catastrophes, or the moral dilemmas of wielding great power. Show the stakes through the effects on the world and characters.

- o Example:

  - As the mage whispered the incantation, the air around her crackled with energy. The grass beneath her feet turned black, and the ground began to quake. "This is too much power," she whispered, her voice trembling.

Practical Exercises

1. **Tension Writing Prompts**

- o Write a scene where a character is hiding from someone or something. Focus on sensory details like sounds, shadows, and physical sensations to build suspense.

- o Create a dialogue between two characters where one knows a secret but can't reveal it. Let the tension build through subtext.

2. **Rewrite a Scene**

- o Take a straightforward scene (e.g., a character walking into a room) and rewrite it

with escalating tension. Use physical
reactions, setting, and sensory details to
create suspense.

3. **Layered Conflict Practice**

   o   Write a scene where a character faces both
       an external challenge (e.g., being locked in a
       room) and an internal one (e.g.,
       claustrophobia). Show how the two conflicts
       feed into each other.

Examples of Escalating Conflict

1. **Basic Conflict:**

   o   A character needs to deliver a package to
       save their friend.
       Escalation:

   o   They get lost. It starts raining, ruining their
       map. They're followed by a mysterious
       figure who may or may not be dangerous.

2. **Basic Conflict:**

   o   Two rivals meet at a high-stakes
       competition.
       Escalation:

   o   One discovers the other has sabotaged them.
       Then they learn the judges are biased. To top
       it off, they have to work together to solve a
       new, unexpected crisis.

Why Tension and Suspense Matter

Suspense is the glue that holds a reader's attention, while tension provides the highs and lows that keep a story engaging. Together, they create an emotional rollercoaster that ensures readers are emotionally invested in your story. By showing the stakes subtly and mastering the art of escalating conflict, you can craft scenes that linger in the minds of your audience long after they've turned the last page.

Exercises: Writing Emotional Scenes

Transforming "Telling" Passages into "Showing"

Writing emotional scenes effectively is a cornerstone of compelling storytelling. To fully immerse readers in your narrative, you must move beyond simply telling them how a character feels and show the emotions through physical reactions, internal thoughts, dialogue, and interactions with the environment. The exercises below are designed to help you practice this skill by transforming "telling" passages into vivid, engaging "showing" moments.

Understanding "Telling" vs. "Showing"

Before diving into the exercises, let's look at a quick comparison:

- **Telling**: "She was sad about the breakup."

- **Showing**: "Her hand lingered on the empty side of the bed, her fingers curling into the cold sheets. She bit her lip to keep the sobs from spilling out, but her chest tightened with every breath."

The difference lies in how much detail and engagement the reader gets. Showing invites the audience into the moment, allowing them to experience the emotion alongside the character.

Exercise 1: Physical Reactions

Objective: Use body language and physical cues to convey emotion.

1. **Step 1**: Start with a "telling" statement.
   Example: "He was terrified of the dark basement."

2. **Step 2**: Rewrite it to show his fear using physical reactions.
   Example: "He gripped the flashlight so tightly his knuckles turned white. The beam shook as he stepped onto the first creaking stair. His breath came in shallow gasps, and a bead of sweat trickled down his temple."

Practice Prompt:
Rewrite the following "telling" sentences into "showing":

- "She was furious at her friend."

- "He felt nervous about the interview."

- "The child was excited for her birthday party."

Exercise 2: Internal Thoughts and Subtext

Objective: Show emotions through a character's internal monologue or subtext in dialogue.

1. **Step 1**: Begin with a "telling" statement.
    Example: "She felt guilty for lying."

2. **Step 2**: Rewrite the passage to include internal thoughts.
    Example: "The words tasted bitter on her tongue, but it was too late to take them back. She glanced at his trusting eyes and felt a hollow ache in her chest. Why couldn't she just tell him the truth?"

3. **Step 3**: Layer the internal thoughts with subtext if appropriate.
    Example: Instead of saying, "I lied to you," she might say, "I didn't mean for things to happen this way," leaving the listener to infer her guilt.

Practice Prompt:
Write a scene showing these emotions through internal thoughts or subtext:

- Regret after making a mistake.

- Joy at reuniting with a loved one.

- Anxiety before a difficult decision.

Exercise 3: Sensory Details

Objective: Engage the five senses to enhance the emotional impact of a scene.

1. **Step 1**: Choose an emotion to focus on.
    Example: Fear.

2. **Step 2**: Create a scene that uses at least three senses to convey that emotion.
    Example: "The hallway smelled of damp earth and

decay. Every step echoed in the suffocating silence, amplifying her growing dread. Her fingers brushed against the rough, crumbling walls as she groped her way forward, the darkness pressing in like a living thing."

Practice Prompt:
Write scenes that incorporate sensory details for the following emotions:

- Love (e.g., a first kiss).

- Grief (e.g., attending a funeral).

- Anger (e.g., during an argument).

Exercise 4: Dialogue with Emotion

Objective: Use dialogue to convey emotional states without explicitly naming the emotion.

1. **Step 1**: Create a basic dialogue exchange.
   Example:

     o Character A: "I can't believe you did this."

     o Character B: "I didn't have a choice."

2. **Step 2**: Add emotional subtext through tone, pacing, and word choice.
   Example:

     o Character A: "You knew exactly what this would do to me." Her voice cracked, barely louder than a whisper.

- o Character B: "You think I wanted this?" He looked away, jaw clenched, his fingers drumming nervously on the table.

Practice Prompt:
Write a dialogue where characters express the following emotions without stating them outright:

- Betrayal.

- Forgiveness.

- Hope.

Exercise 5: Environmental Interaction

Objective: Use a character's interaction with their environment to reflect their emotional state.

1. **Step 1**: Start with a "telling" statement.
   Example: "He was angry after the argument."

2. **Step 2**: Show the anger through how he interacts with his surroundings.
   Example: "He stormed into the kitchen, yanking open the fridge door. Bottles clinked as he grabbed a drink, his grip so tight he nearly crushed the can. When it slipped, spilling soda across the counter, he slammed his fist down, sending a spoon clattering to the floor."

Practice Prompt:
Write scenes showing emotions through environmental interactions:

- Sadness (e.g., sitting alone in a quiet room).

- Frustration (e.g., failing to fix something).

- Happiness (e.g., exploring a favorite place).

-

Exercise 6: Combining Techniques

Objective: Combine multiple techniques to craft a fully realized emotional scene.

Prompt:
Write a scene in which a character receives life-changing news. Use a combination of:

- Physical reactions.

- Internal thoughts.

- Dialogue.

- Sensory details.

- Interaction with the environment.

Example Response:

- The phone slipped from her hand, hitting the floor with a sharp crack. For a moment, the world seemed to stop, the words she'd just heard echoing in her mind like a distant thunderclap. She pressed her trembling hand to her mouth, her knees buckling as she sank into the chair. "No… no, that can't be right," she whispered to no one, her voice hoarse. Outside the window, the rain continued to fall, a relentless rhythm against the glass that matched the pounding of her heart.

Exercise 7: Rewrite Telling into Showing

Objective: Transform provided "telling" passages into vivid "showing" scenes.

Telling Passages:

1. "He was devastated by the loss of his dog."

2. "She was overjoyed to win the competition."

3. "The storm frightened the children."

Practice Task: Rewrite each passage to show the emotions through actions, sensory details, and dialogue.

Example Response for #1:

- "The leash hung limp in his hand, its bright red fabric now faded and frayed at the edges. He dropped it onto the empty dog bed and stared at it for what felt like hours. The silence in the house was deafening—no nails clicking on the hardwood, no soft huffs from the corner. His chest tightened, and he sank onto the couch, burying his face in his hands as the tears finally came."

Exercise 8: Emotional Arc Practice

Objective: Show a progression of emotions within a single scene.

Prompt:
Write a scene where a character starts in one emotional state and transitions to another. For example:

- From despair to hope.

- From anger to regret.

- From confusion to understanding.

Tips:

- Use physical reactions and internal thoughts to show the shift.

- Include dialogue or environmental changes to reinforce the transition.

Why These Exercises Matter

These exercises focus on the nuances of showing emotions, helping you to move away from surface-level descriptions and engage readers more deeply. By practicing these techniques, you'll develop a stronger command of emotional storytelling, enriching your characters and scenes with authenticity and depth. Through consistent effort and revision, you'll learn to trust your ability to show rather than tell, creating an immersive experience that resonates with your audience.

Chapter Six

Structuring Your Narrative

Pacing and Showing: Balancing Narrative Flow

Pacing is the rhythm of your narrative—the speed at which your story unfolds. A well-paced story alternates between slower, immersive scenes and faster, concise summaries to keep readers engaged. The way you choose to show rather than tell directly impacts this pacing. Showing immerses the reader in vivid, detailed scenes, while telling can efficiently convey essential information without slowing down the narrative unnecessarily. This chapter explores how to use showing effectively to control pacing and strike the right balance.

How Showing Impacts Narrative Flow

Immersive Storytelling

Showing allows readers to experience the world and emotions of your story alongside the characters. By revealing details through actions, dialogue, and sensory descriptions, you draw readers into the moment, creating a sense of immediacy and presence.

Example of Showing:

- Instead of telling, "The battlefield was chaotic," show:
    - "Smoke curled through the air, stinging his eyes and filling his lungs with acrid

> bitterness. Screams mingled with the clash
> of steel, and the ground beneath him
> trembled with the weight of charging
> horses."

This level of detail slows the pace but enriches the scene, allowing readers to visualize and feel the chaos.

Building Emotional Stakes

Showing is particularly powerful in moments of high emotional intensity. By describing physical reactions, internal thoughts, and subtext, you help readers connect with your characters' experiences on a deeper level.

Example of Emotional Showing:

- **Telling:** "She was heartbroken when she found out he had lied to her."

- **Showing:** "Her hand hovered over the text message, her eyes scanning the words over and over. The pit in her stomach grew heavier with each read. She dropped the phone onto the couch, pressing her palms into her eyes as if to block out the truth."

By fully immersing the reader, showing can slow the pace, creating space for reflection and emotional engagement.

Balancing Slow, Immersive Scenes with Quicker Summaries

Too much showing can bog down your narrative, overwhelming readers with excessive detail. Conversely, relying too much on telling can make the story feel rushed or flat. The key to effective pacing lies in balancing these techniques.

When to Show

1. **Key Emotional Moments**

   o Show when emotions are running high or when a character faces a critical decision. These moments benefit from the depth and intensity of showing.

2. **Crucial Turning Points**

   o For pivotal scenes that change the course of the story, showing allows readers to fully grasp the stakes and implications.

3. **Character Development**

   o Use showing to reveal traits, motivations, and conflicts subtly. Actions, dialogue, and reactions paint a vivid picture of who your characters are.

4. **Atmosphere and Tone**

   o Show details to set the mood or tone, especially in establishing settings that are integral to the story.

When to Tell

1. **Transitions**

   o Use telling to bridge scenes or summarize less critical events. For example: "Over the next week, the town buzzed with preparations for the festival."

2. Background Information

- o Telling can efficiently convey backstory or context without derailing the narrative flow. For example: "He had spent years training as a soldier, honing his skills for moments like this."

3. Unimportant Details

- o For minor events or actions that don't require emotional depth, telling keeps the story moving. For instance: "She packed her bag and headed to the station."

Finding the Balance

Think of your narrative as a symphony. Showing is the solo performance that holds the spotlight, while telling is the steady rhythm that maintains momentum. Too much of one risks creating either a tedious or shallow experience.

Example of Balance:

- **Unbalanced Showing:**
  - o "She woke up to the sound of her alarm clock blaring in her ear. Rolling over, she slapped the snooze button and sighed, letting the stillness of the morning wash over her. She stared at the ceiling, counting the cracks in the paint, before finally throwing off the covers and dragging herself out of bed. The floor was cold under her feet as she shuffled to the bathroom."

- o   This is overly detailed for a routine action and slows the story unnecessarily.

- **Balanced Approach:**

  - o   "The alarm blared, and she groaned, throwing off the covers. The day loomed ahead, heavy with unspoken promises and fears."

  - o   Here, the details are pared down, yet the emotional tone is conveyed.

Techniques for Controlling Pacing with Showing

1. Vary Sentence Length and Structure

- Short, fragmented sentences create urgency and quicken the pace.

  - o   Example: "He ran. The footsteps grew louder. A door slammed ahead."

- Longer, more descriptive sentences slow the pace, encouraging reflection.

  - o   Example: "The sun dipped below the horizon, casting long, golden shadows that stretched across the field, igniting the trees with a fiery glow."

2. Use Showing to Layer Conflict

- Build tension by showing multiple layers of conflict—external and internal.

- o Example: "She nodded, smiling as he handed her the report. But her fingers trembled when she placed it on the desk. The words on the page blurred, and her stomach twisted. She couldn't tell him the truth—not yet."

This slows the scene to focus on her internal struggle, deepening the tension.

3. Tighten Showing in Action Scenes

- In fast-paced action, limit sensory detail to maintain momentum. Focus on immediate reactions and essential imagery.

  - o Example: "The blade flashed in the moonlight. She ducked, the wind of its swing brushing her cheek. Rolling to her feet, she grabbed the nearest rock and hurled it."

This keeps the scene moving while still showing enough detail for the reader to visualize.

4. Use Dialogue and Subtext

- Showing through dialogue can quicken the pace while revealing emotions and stakes.

  - o Example:

    - "You're late," she said, crossing her arms.

    - "I know. I got held up." He avoided her eyes, shifting on his feet.

- "Again?" Her voice was tight, but the tremor betrayed her disappointment.

Exercises for Practicing Pacing with Showing

Exercise 1: Rewrite for Pacing

Take a "telling" summary and rewrite it as an immersive scene, focusing on showing. Then, experiment with tightening the scene to quicken the pace.

- Original: "She was nervous about the interview."

- Rewrite with Showing:

    - "Her hands trembled as she smoothed the wrinkles in her skirt. She rehearsed her opening lines under her breath, her voice barely audible over the pounding in her ears."

- Tightened Version:

    - "She smoothed her skirt, took a deep breath, and stepped into the room. Her heartbeat thundered, but she forced a smile."

Exercise 2: Identify When to Show and Tell

Choose a scene from your story and highlight where you are showing versus telling. Analyze if the pacing feels right or if adjustments are needed.

Exercise 3: Layered Showing

Write a scene where a character faces an external conflict (e.g., a car breaking down) while experiencing an internal struggle (e.g., fear of being late for an important event). Show both conflicts without explicitly stating them.

Conclusion

The way you balance showing and telling significantly influences your story's pacing. By mastering the art of showing, you can immerse readers in crucial moments and slow the pace when needed. At the same time, knowing when to tell ensures that your narrative doesn't get bogged down with unnecessary details. With deliberate practice and a keen eye for narrative rhythm, you can create a story that flows seamlessly, keeping readers engaged from beginning to end.

Building Atmosphere and Mood

Creating an engaging atmosphere and mood is essential for immersing readers in your story. Atmosphere refers to the overall feeling or environment of a scene, while mood is the emotional response it evokes in readers. By showing rather than telling, you can subtly build these elements through tone, rhythm, recurring imagery, and themes. This chapter explores techniques to master these tools for a compelling narrative experience.

Showing Through Tone and Rhythm

Tone and rhythm are foundational to building atmosphere and mood. The tone conveys the writer's attitude toward the subject, while rhythm creates a cadence that can enhance the scene's emotional impact. Together, they set the stage for how readers interpret and experience the narrative.

1. Tone Through Word Choice

The language you use heavily influences the tone. Words carry connotations—emotional or cultural associations—that shape how a scene feels.

- **Example 1: A Creepy Forest**

    o   Telling: "The forest was scary."

    o   Showing: "Twisted branches clawed at the moonlit sky, their skeletal fingers trembling in the cold wind."

    o   The word "clawed" suggests aggression, while "skeletal" evokes death, creating a menacing tone.

- **Example 2: A Peaceful Meadow**

    o   Telling: "The meadow was calming."

    o   Showing: "Wildflowers swayed lazily in the breeze, their vibrant colors splashed across the green expanse like a painter's masterpiece."

    o   Words like "swayed" and "lazily" create a relaxed tone, inviting the reader to feel at ease.

2. Rhythm Through Sentence Structure

The rhythm of your prose can influence the atmosphere. Short, fragmented sentences quicken the pace and build tension, while longer, flowing sentences create a sense of calm or introspection.

- **Fast-Paced Rhythm (Tension):**
    - "The door creaked. Footsteps. Closer. She pressed against the wall, her breath shallow."
    - This staccato rhythm mirrors the character's panic and urgency.

- **Slow-Paced Rhythm (Serenity):**
    - "The waves lapped gently at the shore, their steady rhythm blending with the rustle of leaves in the warm afternoon breeze."
    - Longer sentences and softer sounds slow the pace, evoking tranquility.

3. Combining Tone and Rhythm

Tone and rhythm work best together. For example, a stormy scene might use harsh, jarring words ("splintered branches," "howling winds") combined with quick, punchy sentences to build a chaotic atmosphere.

Using Recurring Imagery and Themes

Recurring imagery and themes help create a cohesive atmosphere throughout your story. By weaving these elements into multiple scenes, you subtly reinforce the mood and tone, deepening the reader's emotional engagement.

1. Recurring Imagery

Imagery refers to vivid, descriptive language that appeals to the senses. Repeating specific images can evoke a consistent mood or tie together disparate parts of your story.

- **Example: Darkness as Imagery**
    - If darkness represents fear or mystery, you can show it in various ways:
        - "Shadows stretched long and thin, swallowing the light."
        - "The flickering candle barely kept the encroaching darkness at bay."
        - "A suffocating blackness filled the room, pressing against her chest."

By using similar imagery in key moments, you create an underlying sense of continuity and atmosphere.

2. Symbolic Imagery

Symbols carry deeper meanings that resonate with the story's themes. Incorporating symbolic imagery can add layers to the atmosphere.

- **Example: Rain as a Symbol**
    - Sadness: "The rain drummed against the window, tracing patterns on the glass like silent tears."
    - Renewal: "The rain washed over the dusty streets, leaving everything fresh and glistening in the sunlight."

3. Themes and Atmosphere

Themes provide a framework for the recurring images and motifs in your story. For example, a theme of loss might use imagery like faded photographs, empty rooms, or withered flowers to evoke a melancholy atmosphere.

- **Example:**

    - Theme: Isolation

    - Recurring Imagery: Bare trees, empty chairs, distant horizons

    - Effect: A pervasive sense of loneliness and separation from others

Practical Techniques for Building Atmosphere and Mood

1. Leverage Setting

Your setting is a natural tool for shaping atmosphere. By describing the environment with specific details, you can establish the tone and mood without overtly stating it.

- **Example: A Haunted House**

    - Telling: "The house was creepy."

    - Showing: "Peeling wallpaper hung in jagged strips, revealing dark stains beneath. The air smelled of mildew and decay, and each step on the rotting floorboards echoed like a ghost's whisper."

2. Character Perception

The way characters interact with their surroundings can reveal mood and atmosphere. A nervous character might notice shadows and creaks in a house, while a confident one might dismiss these as quirks of an old building.

- **Example:**
    - Nervous: "Her fingers hovered over the doorknob, her breath catching as a faint creak echoed through the hall."
    - Confident: "He pushed open the creaky door, chuckling at the overly dramatic stories about the place."

3. Use Weather and Natural Elements

Weather often mirrors or enhances the mood of a scene. A storm can amplify tension, while sunlight can soften an emotional moment.

- **Example:**
    - Tension: "Thunder growled in the distance, and the wind whipped at her coat, driving icy needles of rain into her skin."
    - Relief: "Golden sunlight broke through the clouds, warming her face and lighting up the world with renewed color."

4. Employ Contrast

Contrast can make an atmosphere more striking. Pairing opposing elements—like a cheerful setting with an ominous tone—creates a sense of unease.

- **Example:**

    - "The playground stood empty, the swings swaying gently in the breeze. Laughter still echoed faintly in the air, but the silence felt heavy, unnatural."

Exercises for Practicing Atmosphere and Mood

Exercise 1: Tone Through Word Choice

Write a description of the same setting using two different tones. For example, describe a forest as peaceful and then as menacing.

- **Peaceful Tone:**

    - "Sunlight filtered through the leafy canopy, casting soft dappled patterns on the mossy ground. Birds chirped in a gentle rhythm, blending with the rustle of the breeze."

- **Menacing Tone:**

    - "Branches twisted together overhead, blotting out the sun. The forest floor was a tangle of roots and shadows, and every snap of a twig sounded like a warning."

Exercise 2: Symbolic Imagery

Choose a theme (e.g., freedom, fear, love) and brainstorm three symbols or images that could represent it. Write a short paragraph incorporating one of those symbols to convey the theme.

Exercise 3: Rhythm in Prose

Write a scene with two versions of pacing. First, use short, choppy sentences to create tension. Then, rewrite the scene with longer, flowing sentences to create calm.

Exercise 4: Recurring Imagery

Identify a recurring image you could use in a story (e.g., shadows, mirrors, fire). Write three descriptions of different scenes that incorporate this imagery to reinforce the mood.

Exercise 5: Contrast in Atmosphere

Write a scene where the setting contrasts with the mood of the character. For example, a cheerful carnival where the protagonist feels dread.

Why Atmosphere and Mood Matter

Atmosphere and mood are what transform a good story into a memorable one. They envelop readers in the world of your narrative, making them feel the emotions and stakes alongside your characters. By showing rather than telling through tone, rhythm, recurring imagery, and themes, you invite readers to experience the story on a visceral level. Mastering these techniques will not only enhance your storytelling but also ensure your work leaves a lasting impression.

Chapter Seven

Polishing Your Writing

Editing for Show, Don't Tell

Mastering "show, don't tell" often comes down to careful editing. Even experienced writers may inadvertently rely on telling in their initial drafts. Revising your work with a focus on transforming telling into showing can elevate your narrative, making it more immersive and emotionally engaging. This chapter explores techniques for identifying "telling" sentences, revising them effectively, and using tools to improve your editing process.

Identifying "Telling" Sentences

What to Look For

Telling sentences often lack detail and fail to engage the reader's senses or emotions. Here are common signs of telling:

1. **Flat Statements of Emotion**

   o   Example: "She was sad."

   o   Why it's telling: It states the character's emotion without showing how it manifests.

2. **Explanations of a Character's State or Motivation**

   o   Example: "He wanted to impress her."

o   Why it's telling: It summarizes rather than demonstrating the character's actions or thoughts.

3. **Overt Descriptions of Setting**

    o   Example: "The house was creepy."

    o   Why it's telling: It doesn't provide sensory details to convey the atmosphere.

4. **Summaries of Events**

    o   Example: "He spent the afternoon cleaning."

    o   Why it's telling: It glosses over what could be a scene that reveals character or conflict.

How to Spot Telling in Your Draft

1. **Highlight Emotional Words**

    o   Look for words like "angry," "sad," "happy," "scared," or "excited." These can signal places where you may be telling rather than showing.

2. **Scan for Overused Verbs**

    o   Verbs like "was," "felt," "wanted," or "had" can indicate telling. While these verbs aren't inherently bad, over-reliance on them may weaken your narrative.

3. **Ask, "Can I Picture This?"**

    o   If a sentence doesn't evoke a clear image or sensory experience, it may need to be reworked.

Revising "Telling" into "Showing"

Once you've identified telling sentences, the next step is to revise them. Here's how to transform flat descriptions into vivid, engaging prose.

1. Add Sensory Details

Bring scenes to life by describing what characters see, hear, smell, taste, or feel.

- **Telling:** "The room smelled bad."

- **Showing:** "The sour stench of rotting garbage hung in the air, making her stomach churn."

2. Use Body Language and Actions

Characters' physical reactions can convey emotions more powerfully than naming the emotion.

- **Telling:** "He was nervous about the presentation."

- **Showing:** "His hands shook as he adjusted the microphone, and his voice cracked on the first word."

3. Incorporate Internal Thoughts

Let readers into your characters' minds to reveal their emotions and motivations.

- **Telling:** "She wanted to escape."

- **Showing:** "Her eyes darted to the door, calculating the steps it would take to get there without being noticed."

4. Use Subtext in Dialogue

Instead of stating emotions outright, let characters reveal their feelings through subtext and tone.

- **Telling:** "She was angry at him."
- **Showing:**
    - "You forgot again," she said, her voice low and steady, though her fingers gripped the edge of the table until her knuckles turned white.

5. Expand Key Moments

If a summary glosses over an important event or emotion, expand it into a full scene.

- **Telling:** "He spent the afternoon cleaning."
- **Showing:**
    - "Sweat dripped from his brow as he scrubbed the kitchen tiles, the sponge worn thin in his hand. He attacked the grease-stained counters with a vengeance, as if cleaning away the mess could undo the argument from earlier."

Tools for Self-Editing

Editing for "show, don't tell" requires a keen eye and some methodical tools. These techniques will help you refine your prose and develop the skill to spot areas for improvement.

1. The "Show, Don't Tell" Checklist

Use this checklist as you review your draft:

- Does this sentence evoke an image, feeling, or sensory detail?

- Is the character's emotion revealed through actions, dialogue, or thoughts?

- Are the stakes or motivations implied rather than explained?

- Can I replace a summary with a vivid description?

2. Use Highlighters for Telling Words

Print your manuscript and highlight instances of telling words (e.g., "was," "felt," "wanted," "happy"). This visual approach makes it easier to spot patterns of telling.

3. Reverse Engineering

Look at a scene and rewrite it in two ways: one with pure telling and one with immersive showing. Compare the impact of each version.

- Example:

    o **Telling:** "He was cold."

    o **Showing:** "The icy wind bit at his cheeks, and his breath fogged the air with every exhale."

4. Read Aloud

Hearing your prose can help you identify flat or unengaging passages. If a sentence feels bland or doesn't evoke a reaction, it might be telling rather than showing.

5. Use Beta Readers

Ask trusted readers to identify parts of the story where they feel disconnected or uninvolved. These areas might benefit from more showing.

6. Employ Editing Software

Tools like ProWritingAid or Hemingway Editor can flag weak verbs, overly simple sentences, or areas where your writing lacks depth. While not perfect, these programs can serve as a starting point for revisions.

7. Keep a "Show, Don't Tell" Journal

Practice makes perfect. Dedicate a notebook or digital document to rewriting telling sentences into showing ones. Over time, you'll naturally start incorporating more showing into your first drafts.

Examples of Before and After

Example 1: Emotions

- **Before (Telling):** "She was terrified."

- **After (Showing):** "Her breath came in short, sharp bursts, and her legs felt like they might give out as she stumbled backward, her eyes fixed on the shadow in the corner."

Example 2: Setting

- **Before (Telling):** "The city was beautiful at night."

- **After (Showing):** "Neon lights reflected off wet pavement, painting the streets in streaks of red, blue, and gold. The hum of distant music mingled with the chatter of late-night diners spilling out of crowded cafes."

Example 3: Character Motivation

- **Before (Telling):** "He wanted to prove himself."

- **After (Showing):** "He stayed long after the others had left, his fingers aching from gripping the wrench. When the machine finally roared to life, a tired but triumphant smile spread across his face."

Common Pitfalls to Avoid

1. **Overwriting**

   - Showing doesn't mean describing every detail. Focus on the most impactful elements.

   - Overwritten: "Her eyes welled with tears, her shoulders slumped, and she let out a long, shuddering sigh, her fingers gripping the edge of the table as she leaned forward, overwhelmed by the weight of her sadness."

   - Streamlined: "Her shoulders slumped as a single tear traced a path down her cheek."

2. **Forgetting to Balance**

   - Not every sentence needs to be a masterclass in showing. Use telling judiciously for transitions or unimportant details.

   -

3. **Unclear Showing**

- o   Be sure your showing is clear and understandable. Ambiguity can confuse readers if not done intentionally.

Conclusion

Editing for "show, don't tell" is a transformative step in the writing process. By identifying telling sentences and revising them into vivid, engaging prose, you can create a story that resonates with readers. With practice, the techniques and tools outlined here will become second nature, allowing you to craft immersive narratives that leave a lasting impact.

Final Checklist: A Quick-Reference Guide for Spotting Opportunities to Show

Editing for "show, don't tell" can feel overwhelming, especially when revisiting an entire manuscript. This final checklist serves as a streamlined tool to help you quickly identify and revise areas where showing could enhance your narrative. Keep it handy as you edit to ensure your story is engaging, vivid, and immersive.

1. Emotional States

- **Check for:** Words like "happy," "sad," "angry," "scared," or "nervous."

  - o   These often indicate telling by summarizing the character's feelings.

- **Ask yourself:** How can I show this emotion through physical reactions, dialogue, or internal thoughts?

- **Example:**

  - **Telling:** "She was nervous about the speech."

  - **Showing:** "She gripped the edges of the podium, her knuckles white, and cleared her throat twice before the words finally came out."

2. Physical Descriptions

- **Check for:** Generic descriptions like "The room was messy" or "The forest was beautiful."

- **Ask yourself:** Can I add sensory details to immerse the reader? What does the character see, smell, hear, or feel in this moment?

- **Example:**

  - **Telling:** "The kitchen was messy."

  - **Showing:** "Unwashed dishes teetered precariously in the sink, and the sticky countertop smelled faintly of sour milk."

3. Character Motivations

- **Check for:** Sentences that explain what a character wants or why they're acting in a certain way.

- o Look for phrases like "He wanted," "She needed," or "They felt."

- **Ask yourself:** Can I show the motivation through the character's actions or internal thoughts instead of stating it outright?

- **Example:**

  - o **Telling:** "He wanted to prove he was brave."

  - o **Showing:** "He tightened his grip on the sword, his hands shaking, and stepped into the dark cave despite the lump of fear lodged in his throat."

4. Dialogue and Subtext

- **Check for:** Dialogue tags like "she said angrily" or "he replied sadly."

  - o These often tell the reader how a character feels instead of showing it through their words, tone, or actions.

- **Ask yourself:** Can the dialogue itself reveal the emotion? How can I add subtext or body language to enhance it?

- **Example:**

  - o **Telling:** "I don't care," she said angrily.

  - o **Showing:** "I don't care." Her voice was sharp, and her fist slammed onto the table.

5. Transitions and Summaries

- **Check for:** Sections that summarize actions or events, especially during key moments.

    - Phrases like "They spent the day preparing" or "She thought about her choices" might miss opportunities for depth.

- **Ask yourself:** Is this a moment worth expanding into a scene? If not, is the summary engaging and clear?

- **Example:**

    - **Telling:** "They spent hours preparing the party."

    - **Showing:** "Balloons popped as they scrambled to tie them, frosting smudged on their noses, and the room filled with bursts of laughter as streamers fell off the walls."

6. Pacing Balance

- **Check for:** Overly detailed passages that slow the story or summaries that skip over key emotional beats.

- **Ask yourself:** Is the level of detail appropriate for the scene? Am I showing where it matters most?

- **Tip:** Use telling sparingly for minor actions or transitions, saving showing for pivotal moments.

Editing Workflow with This Checklist

1. **Start Broad:** Focus on high-impact scenes first—moments of conflict, emotional intensity, or key turning points. These are the places where showing has the most impact.

2. **Work Scene by Scene:** Apply the checklist to each scene, looking for opportunities to show emotions, settings, or character motivations.

3. **Tackle Dialogue:** Review your dialogue and tags, ensuring the emotional subtext comes through naturally.

4. **Polish Transitions:** For less critical moments, simplify telling to maintain narrative flow while avoiding flat prose.

This quick-reference guide is your go-to tool for enhancing your prose. By systematically applying it, you can refine your manuscript into a vivid, engaging story that pulls readers into every moment.

Chapter Eight

Advanced Techniques

Subtext in Storytelling

Subtext is the unspoken or hidden meaning beneath the surface of a narrative. It enriches a story by allowing readers to infer deeper layers of meaning, making the experience more engaging and thought-provoking. When used effectively, subtext weaves themes, emotions, and symbolism into your story, creating a rich tapestry of meaning that goes beyond the literal events on the page. This section explores how to use subtext to craft nuanced storytelling and provides techniques for symbolic showing.

Weaving Deeper Meanings into Your Narrative

1. Understanding Subtext

Subtext exists in the spaces between the lines, where the unsaid or implied becomes as important as the stated. It invites readers to engage actively, interpreting clues and uncovering themes.

- **Example:**

  - **Surface Level:** A character sits silently at the dinner table.

  - **Subtext:** The silence represents unspoken tension, unresolved conflict, or fear of confrontation.

Subtext transforms simple scenes into complex moments, allowing readers to feel the undercurrents without being directly told.

2. Using Subtext to Reflect Themes

Subtext can reinforce your story's central themes subtly, ensuring they resonate without being overtly stated.

- **Example:** A story about the consequences of greed might feature a recurring motif of deteriorating objects, such as a cracked mirror or a fading painting. These symbols reflect the decay greed brings without stating it outright.

3. Implied Emotions in Characters

Characters can express emotions indirectly through their actions, dialogue, or body language, allowing subtext to convey deeper feelings.

- **Example:**
  - **Telling:** "She was angry at him."
  - **Subtextual Showing:** She picked up the broken vase and set it on the table without a word, her lips pressed into a thin line.

Here, the character's anger is clear through her restrained actions, creating tension and nuance.

Techniques for Symbolic Showing

1. Symbolism Through Objects

Objects can carry symbolic weight, representing larger ideas or emotions. By showing how characters interact with these objects, you can create layers of meaning.

- **Example:** A wedding ring might symbolize commitment, regret, or entrapment, depending on how it's described:

    - Commitment: "She slipped the ring onto her finger, her heart swelling with hope."

    - Regret: "The ring felt heavy on her hand, its gold dull in the dim light."

    - Entrapment: "She twisted the ring around her finger, as if testing the strength of invisible chains."

2. Recurring Imagery

Repeating specific images or motifs can subtly reinforce themes or emotions throughout the story.

- **Example:** In a story about resilience, recurring images of cracked but unbroken objects—like a damaged but standing tree—can symbolize strength in adversity.

3. Contrast and Juxtaposition

Using contrast between a character's words and actions creates subtext. For example:

- **Dialogue:** "I'm fine."

- **Action:** The character's hands tremble as they avoid eye contact.

This contrast reveals the true emotional state without explicitly stating it.

Practice Exercise

Write a scene where two characters discuss a mundane topic (e.g., the weather) while subtext reveals underlying tension, attraction, or conflict. Focus on body language, tone, and symbolic details to convey the deeper meaning.

By mastering subtext, you'll create stories that resonate long after the final page, engaging readers on multiple levels and inviting them to uncover the layers hidden beneath the surface.

Foreshadowing Through Showing

Foreshadowing is a powerful narrative tool that plants subtle hints about future events, creating anticipation and intrigue. When done through showing, foreshadowing becomes an immersive experience for readers, blending seamlessly into the story and adding layers of meaning. This section explores how to use subtle hints effectively and discusses their impact on the reader's experience.

The Purpose of Foreshadowing

Foreshadowing serves multiple purposes in storytelling:

1. **Builds Anticipation**: It creates a sense of suspense, encouraging readers to keep turning the pages to uncover what happens next.

2. **Enhances Re-Reads**: Subtle hints become satisfying Easter eggs for readers who revisit your story, deepening their appreciation for the narrative.

3. **Reinforces Themes**: Foreshadowing can underscore key themes, making the story feel cohesive and deliberate.

4. **Prepares Readers**: It primes readers for upcoming events, ensuring that major twists or developments feel earned rather than abrupt.

By showing rather than telling, foreshadowing becomes an art of implication, allowing readers to infer possibilities without being explicitly told what lies ahead.

Subtle Hints: How to Show Foreshadowing

1. Use Symbolism

Symbols can foreshadow events or themes without being overt. An object, setting, or recurring motif can hint at what's to come.

- **Example:** A cracked mirror seen early in the story might foreshadow the eventual fracturing of a character's identity or relationships.

  - "The mirror in the hallway was split down the center, the two halves distorting her reflection into something unrecognizable."

2. Employ Tone and Atmosphere

Subtle shifts in tone or mood can signal future developments. Changes in the environment or the reactions of secondary characters can create an undercurrent of unease or foreshadow trouble.

- **Example:**

    - "The cheerful bustle of the market seemed to falter for a moment, the laughter fading into an unnatural hush as dark clouds gathered on the horizon."

3. Foreshadow Through Dialogue

Characters' words can contain double meanings or hint at events to come, especially when paired with subtext.

- **Example:**

    - Early in the story:

        - "I've always had a bad feeling about crossing that bridge," she said, laughing nervously.

    - Later in the story:

        - The bridge collapses during a storm, trapping her on the other side.

4. Details in Character Behavior

Small, seemingly inconsequential actions can hint at future conflicts or resolutions.

- **Example:** A character repeatedly fiddling with a locket might foreshadow the significance of its contents in a later reveal.

    - "He turned the locket over in his hand, his thumb tracing the worn engraving, but snapped it shut before anyone could see inside."

5. Use the Environment

The setting itself can foreshadow events. A broken fence might hint at an escape or intrusion, or a withering garden might symbolize a deteriorating relationship.

- **Example:**

    - "The once-thriving roses in the garden had wilted, their petals scattered across the soil like forgotten promises."

The Impact on Readers

Foreshadowing, when done well, enhances the reader's experience in several ways:

1. **Keeps Them Engaged**: Subtle hints spark curiosity, making readers eager to piece together the puzzle.

2. **Creates Emotional Payoff**: When foreshadowed events unfold, readers feel a sense of satisfaction, as if they've been rewarded for their attention to detail.

3. **Strengthens Suspense**: Foreshadowing builds a sense of inevitability, heightening tension as readers anticipate what's to come.

Avoiding Common Pitfalls

1. **Don't Overdo It**: If foreshadowing is too obvious, it can ruin the surprise or make the story feel predictable.

2. **Maintain Subtlety**: Use foreshadowing sparingly and integrate it naturally into the narrative.

3. **Balance Payoff**: Ensure that hints lead to meaningful developments. If foreshadowing doesn't pay off, it can frustrate readers.

Practice Exercise

Write a scene where you subtly foreshadow a major event later in the story. Use one or more techniques (symbolism, tone, dialogue, or setting) to plant hints while keeping the meaning ambiguous.

By mastering the art of foreshadowing through showing, you can create narratives that feel layered, engaging, and deeply satisfying, drawing readers into your story's world and keeping them hooked until the very end.

Balancing Showing with Efficiency

The principle of "show, don't tell" is essential for creating vivid, engaging stories, but it comes with a challenge: avoiding overwriting. While showing immerses readers in the world of your story, overloading your narrative with excessive detail can bog down the pace and exhaust the reader. Striking the right balance means knowing when to elaborate and when to condense while maintaining depth and impact.

Why Overwriting Happens

1. **Desire to Be Thorough**

   o Writers often want to ensure their audience fully understands a character's emotions or a scene's atmosphere. This can lead to over-explaining.

2. **Fear of Reader Misinterpretation**

   o Overwriting stems from a lack of trust in the reader's ability to infer meaning from subtle hints.

3. **Enthusiasm for Description**

   o Sometimes, writers get carried away with descriptive language, adding unnecessary details that detract from the story.

Signs of Overwriting

1. **Redundant Details**

   o If a single idea is conveyed multiple times in slightly different ways, it may be overwriting.

   o **Example:**

     ▪ "Her hands shook, her breath came in short gasps, and her heart raced as fear gripped her chest."

- Revised: "Her hands shook, and her breath came in short gasps, fear gripping her chest."

2. **Lengthy Descriptions of the Mundane**

   o Over-describing trivial actions or objects can disrupt the narrative flow.

   o **Example:**

      - "She grabbed the cup, lifting it slowly to her lips, the steam curling into delicate patterns in the air as the liquid warmed her hands and slid down her throat."

      - Revised: "She sipped her coffee, savoring its warmth."

3. **Unnecessary Adjectives and Adverbs**

   o Too many modifiers can clutter your prose and dilute its impact.

   o **Example:**

      - "The beautifully bright and glowing moonlight illuminated the dark and gloomy forest."

      - Revised: "The moonlight illuminated the gloomy forest."

Techniques for Balancing Showing with Efficiency

1. Prioritize Key Moments

Focus your detailed showing on pivotal scenes—moments of high tension, emotional turning points, or significant revelations. For less critical moments, use concise summaries.

- **Example:**

    - Key Moment (Show): "Tears streamed down her face as she clutched the letter, her fingers trembling over the words that shattered her world."

    - Transition (Tell): "The next week passed in a blur of grief and unanswered questions."

2. Combine Actions and Descriptions

Blend sensory details and character actions into the flow of the narrative to maintain momentum.

- **Example:**

    - Overwritten: "The library was quiet, with rows of towering bookshelves filled with dusty tomes. She walked through the aisles, her footsteps echoing in the silence."

    - Efficient: "Her footsteps echoed through the quiet library, the scent of dusty books filling the air."

3. Trust Your Reader

Imply rather than explain. Readers appreciate subtlety and enjoy uncovering layers of meaning on their own.

- **Example:**

- o Overwritten: "He clenched his fists tightly, his knuckles white, his jaw locked in frustration, and his eyes blazing with anger."

- o Efficient: "He clenched his fists, his jaw tight."

4. Use Dialogue Strategically

Let characters reveal emotions, conflicts, and motivations through dialogue rather than lengthy exposition or internal monologue.

- **Example:**

    - o Overwritten: "She was upset with him for not calling and decided to let him know."

    - o Efficient: "You couldn't pick up the phone once?" she asked, her voice sharp.

Exercises to Practice Efficiency

1. **Rewrite for Brevity**
   Take a passage from your writing and identify redundant details or overly descriptive sentences. Revise it to maintain depth while cutting unnecessary words.

2. **Focus on One Sense**
   Practice describing a scene using details from only one sense (sight, sound, touch, etc.). Then revise by incorporating a second sense sparingly to enhance the scene without overwhelming it.

3. **Condense a Scene**

   Take a 200-word descriptive scene and rewrite it in 100 words without losing the emotional impact.

Why Efficiency Matters

Balancing showing with efficiency ensures your story remains engaging and impactful without overwhelming the reader. By focusing on what matters most and trusting your audience, you can maintain depth and clarity, allowing your narrative to flow seamlessly while immersing readers in the world you've created.